Food
in
Good Season

Food
in
Good Season

by Betty Fussell

Illustrated by Glenna Putt

ALFRED A. KNOPF *New York* 1988

Library of Congress Cataloging-in-Publication Data
Fussell, Betty Harper.
Food in good season.
Includes index.
1. Cookery.   I. Title.
TX715.F977   1988   641.5   88-45352
ISBN 0-394-57117-7

Manufactured in the United States of America
First Edition

I would like to thank Thomas Rawls and John Barstow for launching
most of these pieces, in an earlier form, under the rubric "A Cook's
Tour," in Blair & Ketchum's *Country Journal.* Thanks also to Beverly
Williams for early support and to Wanda Shipman for later editing.
Most of all I would like to thank Glenna Putt for the gift, over these
many years, of her quick eye and skillful hand, her bright intelligence
and imagination, that makes of this little calendar a lifelong collabora-
tion between friends.

For Pat and Don

How many things by season season'd are —

The Merchant of Venice, V, i, 107

CONTENTS

May

June

July

August

September

October

November

December

Bread for All Seasons

Food in Good Season

WATERMELONS FROM
OUR PATCH

Everyone who cooks, and nearly everyone who eats, has an ideal kitchen in his head. Mine is in the country. It is roomy and yet cozy, the heart of a busy house and yet tranquil, a place that welcomes the traffic of children, pets, friends, and workmen, whose footsteps miraculously track no mud. There are windows everywhere, which let in light and look out on green pastures and distant woods. Pots of geraniums and rows of tomatoes redden the windowsills. Bunches of herbs hang from the beams, for of course there *are* beams in this kitchen, and a very large fireplace with a stone hearth, and over the glowing coals of hickory a suckling pig turning, forever, on a spit.

On the plain pine table in the center, a wicker basket holds eggs freshly plucked from the nests of the hens and ducks that scrabble in the yard. A loaf of bread, which has always just been taken from the oven by the hearth, scents the air as it cools. A basket of greens, fresh from the garden, awaits the clear, cool water of the sink. Fuzzy peaches, cherries on their stems, tender raspberries just garnered from the orchard spill in profusion from their baskets because all the foods I love best are, here, always in season. This is an ideal kitchen, remember, where thick cream stands in pails in the dairy, honey flows from the hives, lambs frolic in the pasture, grapes hang heavy in the arbor, trout thicken the stream, mushrooms carpet the woods, partridge and woodcocks crowd the trees, and the sun shines every single day.

In reality, I lived once in a country house with a kitchen where the eighteenth-century fireplace constantly smoked, the well ran dry, the neighbor's goats ate my bushes, his pit bull killed my chickens, a drunken farmer shot and killed the guinea hens in my walnut trees, and in an upstairs bedroom a rat cornered my cat. When I fled the country for the suburbs and planted a garden of herbs and salad greens, fruits and vegetables, now it was my neighbor's Labs and retrievers that trampled my strawberries, his children who ate my tomatoes, and my very own slugs that got the lettuce. When I abandoned the suburbs for the city, and set a row of potted herbs on my sill, their stems drooped and their leaves withered quicker than a thief could pick my lock.

It was ever thus. There are always real nematodes in imaginary gardens. The sunny pastoral of Elizabethan country house cooking, evoked in works like *Elinor Fettiplace's Receipt Book* of 1604, is clouded by the fact that 1604 was a severe plague year and Lady Fettiplace was much occupied in distilling herbs in wine and malmsey for the "imperiall water" she ministered to the hosts of relatives, servants, and villagers more dependent on her medicinal receipts than on her culinary ones. Until this century, the word "receipt" embraced the entire field of husbandry, or the management of all that went on in a country kitchen, house, garden, outbuildings, and in the fields. *Family Receipts* is the title H. L. Barnum of Cincinnati gave to his "Practical Guide for the Husbandman and Housewife" in 1831. His guide contained "a Great Variety of Valuable Recipes," as he said, "Relating to Agriculture, Gardening, Brewery, Cookery, Dairy, Confectionary, Diseases, Farriery, Ingrafting, and the Various Branches of Rural and Domestic Economy."

When we yearn for that Edenic world in which grapes fall from the vines into the vat and cream from the cow into the custard, we forget the flies in the buttermilk, the ants in the ointment, the maggots in the ham. We forget how unremitting and exhausting was the practice of rural and domestic economy. A quick glance at Barnum's receipts can remind us of the realities of a country kitchen as he tells us how to kill ants, remove the taste of turnips from butter or milk, make currant wine, preserve eggs, make cheap and agreeable beer, make hotchpotch of mutton, fry eels, hash venison, cure the whooping cough, make tooth powders, make purgative balls for fever in horses, and write out promissory notes.

When we lament the ways in which we are cut off from nature's seasonal round and long for the green world Spenser dreamt of in *The Shepheard's Calendar,* Virgil in his *Eclogues,* Theocritus in his *Idylls,* we forget nature's seasonal hazards. In winter, warns Lydia Child in *The American Frugal Housewife* of 1833, "do not forget to throw a rug or horse-blanket over your pump; a frozen pump is a comfortless preparation for a winter's breakfast." In summer, she warns, "be very careful of fresh meat": if it can't be cooked soon, it should be salted; if it must be kept overnight, it should be looked to just before bed, "and if there is danger, it should be scalded." Receipts for coping with seasonal change before we banished seasons from our refrigerated, centrally heated, and air-conditioned houses now seem as mysterious as the advice in the 1839 *Genesee Farmer:* "Keep your *summer cheese* in your bed chambers; they enrich the qualities of the atmosphere."

As scientific "progress," in nineteenth-century eyes, overcame nature and its seasonal inconveniences, the husbandman and housewife turned from domestic economy to a somewhat more sinister "domestic manipulation." The term "domestic manipulation," defined by Mrs. E. F. Ellet in her 1872 *New Cyclopaedia of Domestic Economy*, "would include all the manual operations required in a house ... such as partake in a slight degree of a scientific character; thus the operations of Filtering, Decanting, Weighing, Measuring, Bottling, Corking, Unstoppering, Pounding, Heating, Boiling, Distilling, Cementing, etc. etc., will be included; whilst Dusting, Washing, and Scrubbing, though no less in strictness manipulations, will be passed over in silence." Despite all the unsilent manipulations in this brave new kitchen, Mrs. Ellet confessed that a grand puzzle remained—"the difficulty of really getting the ingredients on which the mystery of food manufacture is to be exercised."

Even scientific gardens, it seems, are not exempt from nematodes. Mrs. Ellet complained of adulteration and pollution with the outrage of a *Consumer Reports* article a century later, when she excoriated water thick as soup with "monsters," or pepper adulterated with "warehouse sweepings," or coffee grounds mixed with mahogany sawdust "and no little sand," not to mention brown sugar sullied with dirt or butter polluted with cow's hairs. But even without the deceptions or indifference of dishonest or careless purveyors, "really getting the ingredients"—or, as we would say, "getting real ingredients"—was always a grand puzzle for a cook. As early as 1796, Amelia Simmons, in her *American Cookery*, warns the housewife to look to the butter and to select butter from the middle of the firkin lest the sides be "distasted by the wood." Farm-churned butter reduces Catherine Beecher, in her *American Woman's Home* of 1869, to despair: "This has a cheesy taste, that mouldy, this is flavored with cabbage, and that again with turnip, and another has the strong, sharp savor of rancid animal fat."

Let us clear our minds and palates, then, of sentiment and nostalgia for the country kitchens of the past.

Let us also look with clear eyes at the urban kitchens of the present. Despite technological innovations in which radiation kills the bugs on our peppercorns, microwaves zap our bacon, hydroponic greenhouses defy weather, and jet engines annihilate time, getting the real ingredients— a perfectly ripe peach, a totally fresh shrimp—is still a puzzle. Despite our domestic manipulations, we are still tied to the seasons and, like other animals and vegetables, tied to the cycles of growth and decay. Despite our defiance of the stars and planets to determine our lives, we still order our daily lives by solar and lunar calendars. Although we are more remote than ever from the agricultural year, we still celebrate the quadrant of the solar calendar with midsummer and midwinter feasts at solstices when the sun stands still, and with harvest and vernal festivals at equinoxes when the sun turns. Despite our medical manipulations, our daily breath and our very heartbeats are still tuned to the rhythm of the earth's expansion and contraction and the seas' ebb and flow.

Even in my real Manhattan kitchen, where no plants grow, where I can eat Mexican strawberries in December and iced oysters in July, I still order my cooking life by a country calendar. My calendar, of course, is nothing like Mrs. Ellet's in *The New Cyclopaedia*, where she lists under "Articles in Season for Each Month" the following real ingredients for January:

> *Fish.*—Eels, flounders, haddocks, lampreys, oysters, whitings, clams, muscles, striped bass, salt mackerel, smoked salmon, sardines, anchovies, fish pickled and soused.
> *Meats.*—Beef, mutton, fish, pork, ham, venison, veal, sausages, etc.
> *Poultry and game.*—Capons, fowls, ducks, geese, Scotch grouse, prairie fowls, young rabbits, par-

tridges, pheasants, pigeons, wild birds, turkeys, woodcock, snipe, quails, ducks—canvas back, redhead, broad bill, teal—bear's meat, jugged hare.
Vegetables.—Winter spinach, turnips, potatoes, sweet potatoes, rice, celery, cabbage, parsnips, carrots, dried white beans, beets, dried herbs, garlic, onions, shallots, leeks, mint, mustard, parsley, sage, rosemary, salsify, thyme, etc.
Fruits.—Apples, oranges, dried figs, imported grapes, almonds, raisins, dates, filberts, prunes, hard nuts, Brazil and Madeira-nuts, black-walnuts, hickory-nuts, pecan-nuts, butternuts, chestnuts.

My January season boils down to parsnips, venison, and cranberries. My calendar, however, is merely approximate and my domestic economy in no way cyclopaedic. In my calendar, you'll find turkey in November, but you'll also find beets in March and macaroni in August. Many foods that I love you'll not find at all, because I have selected but a few real foods that are rooted in history and grounded in the American earth that nourishes them and me.

I have chosen foods that are simple and can be simply prepared, foods that are rooted in the winter cellars and spring gardens of a particular place—New England. I wrote about most of these foods, originally, in Blair & Ketchum's *Country Journal,* which was founded by a couple of city men looking for an ideal country place in Vermont. Despite the green mountains for which the state is named, Vermont's pastoral is full of real rocks and bad weather. Where else but New England will fall and spring break your heart with their fragility and winter and summer break your spirit with their strength? And yet, where else will foods by a burning hearth or a cooling stream taste quite so good because so hardly won? In New England the seasons are real.

I think of pumpkins and persimmons, of wild mushrooms and nuts in the fall, of big bowls of hot garlicky chowder in winter, of artichokes and asparagus in spring, of blueberries and bluefish and the sweetest of sweet corn in summer. "Our new paradise of New England," as Francis Higginson called it in the seventeenth century, was anything but. And yet here as in no other place do I feel the tug of the seasons and the joy with which an eighteenth-century husbandman could write, as Thomas Jefferson did in his *Garden Book* in the much gentler landscape of Virginia, "Aug. 31. Watermelons from our patch."

I have ended my calendar year with a section on bread because, of all our foods, bread knows no season. Like a weeded and pruned garden, bread stands for the triumph of man's art over chaotic nature, from the brick ovens of Pompeii to the adobe ovens of the Pueblos and the electric ovens of Manhattan. Everyone who bakes bread, and nearly everyone who eats it, has an ideal bread in his head. Bread substantiates the idea that nature can and must be mediated by art, for bread, with its companion wine, turns mortality around. In both bread and wine, the alchemy of fermentation transmutes base matter into edible or liquid gold, and transforms earth into air by means of water and fire. In both, the fifth element is time, domestically manipulated, to compress and exploit nature's cycles of mutability, of growth and decay. From last year's grain, this year's loaves from our oven; from last year's seeds, this year's watermelons from our patch. As Jefferson wrote in his Calendar of Work in his *Farm Book*, "In September, sow wheat to begin the circle again." In my ideal country kitchen, my loaves of bread are as round and circular as the seasons of the year and the paths of planets and stars that order my life and make it real.

January

January

ROOTING FOR PARSNIPS

Creamed Parsnips and Salt Cod

Glazed Parsnips

Penn's Parsnip Pudding

VENISON FEASTS

Roast Venison in a Paste

Currant-Cranberry Sauce

Roast Venison Loin with Garlic-Chili

Venison Sausage

Grandma's Venison Mincemeat

THE REDSKINNED CRANBERRY

Cranberry Succotash

Cold Cranberry Soup

Cran-Pineapple Relish

Cranberry-Orange Sauce

Cranberry Game Sauce

Cran-Nut Cheesecake

ROOTING FOR PARSNIPS

To get in touch with your roots, try parsnips. Parsnips are those funnel-shaped, yellow-white, peasanty roots obscured on your supermarket counters behind the flashy carrot and the waxed turnip. You suspect them of being all wood and pith, bitter at worst and tasteless at best. Something for the starving Armenians, perhaps, but short of starvation, why bother? Let's stick to friends we know and trust: the carrot, the turnip, and—on cold winter nights—the potato.

It wasn't always like this. Until late in the nineteenth century, the parsnip was the very model of what a root vegetable should be. Listen to Messieurs Vilmorin and Andrieux, in a popular work of the last century, *The Vegetable Garden*, eulogize what has become our most prominent current variety, the Hollow Crown, or Student, parsnip: "Root handsome, long, thick, very clean skinned, with a fine neck surrounded by a circular gutter-like depression, from the centre of which the leaves issue, the root being swollen all round it."

This handsome root had reason to be swollen with pride, if nothing else, because it had been esteemed on the tables of Europe since the time of Tiberian Rome. In the Middle Ages, it reigned supreme over Lenten tables because it was nutritious (high in potassium, calcium, and vitamin A), filling (high in carbohydrates), and delectably sweet. It reigned until a tuber from the New World, the *arriviste* potato, displaced it by being blander and more versatile.

For a couple of centuries, however, the parsnip held its own against the potato, since colonists in the New World planted the root far more eagerly than Europe cultivated the tuber. Because the parsnip is at its best in winter, after a good freeze has turned the root's starch to sugar, parsnips with salt fish saved many a starving Pilgrim Protestant as they had once saved fasting Catholics. And our Protestant colonists were good enough to pass the parsnip on to the Indians, who welcomed it to their hillocks of beans and corn.

Colonists who were not starving turned parsnips into pancakes and puddings, following receipts of the kind William Penn's first wife, Gulielma, inscribed, "Too make a Parsnep puding." "Take sum parsneps," Gulielma wrote in England in the mid-seventeenth century, "and boyle them till thay bee very soft, then mash them very small and picke out the hard peces."

Those hard pieces may have led to the parsnip's decline, for the center of the root goes hard and wooden when it is past its prime. But a young swollen root, with a fine neck and a clean skin and everything handsome about it, should not be blamed for the sins of its elders. In any case, you can cut out the hard pieces of the core after cooking.

The best way to cook the parsnip is to parboil it with the skin on, as you might a potato. Then douse it in cold water and the skin will slip off like wet paper. Once the root is peeled, you can slice it crosswise or lengthwise in narrow strips. You can toss the slices in butter and parsley or glaze them in a little sugar, as you might glaze carrots.

Our nineteenth-century ancestors were fond of mashing parsnips, shaping them in balls, rolling them in flour, and sautéing them in butter to make parsnip fritters, as Fannie Farmer did in her 1896 *Boston Cooking-School Cook Book*. But I'm afraid Miss Fannie signaled the current low status of parsnips when she advised, "They are raised mostly for feeding cattle."

Since the root is both pungent in character and dry in texture, it needs emollients like butter, cream, olive oil, or yoghurt, much as a white potato does. Because it is naturally sweet, it has an affinity for sweeteners like sugar, honey, or maple syrup, much as a sweet potato does, and for related spices like nutmeg, cinnamon, and cloves.

With a food processor you can puree parsnips in a trice and experiment with emollients and flavorings. I sometimes combine parsnips with carrots and turnips, smoothing the puree with yoghurt instead of cream, or flavoring it gently with curry powder and sautéed onions. An unsweetened puree makes a fine creamy vegetable to accompany the Sunday roast or to stand on its own, with the addition of eggs, as a surprising vegetable soufflé. Whether the puree is sweetened or unsweetened, I usually add a few drops of lemon juice because it seems to jack up the taste of a root that wants to stay earthbound. Sherry, Madeira, or cognac will do the same.

In the trio of recipes that follows, I have layered parsnips with salt cod in a cream sauce flavored with onion and garlic to acknowledge their former Lenten glory. I have sliced and glazed them to show off their rich, nutty flavor. And I have pureed them with honey, cream, raisins, and rum to make a pudding in honor of Gulielma and William Penn. The very word *parsnip* comes from the Latin word *pastinaca*, from *pastinvu*, the name of a tool for digging, so as long as we're digging into roots, let's go whole hog. Instead of pitying the poor parsnip, let's root for it.

Creamed Parsnips and Salt Cod

1 pound salt cod
2 pounds parsnips
6 tablespoons butter
2 large onions, diced
4 cloves garlic, minced
4 tablespoons flour
2 cups milk (or half and half)
2 cups diced cheese (Swiss, Gruyère, or
   Cheddar)
½ teaspoon dried thyme
pepper to taste
¼ cup grated Parmesan cheese

Soak cod twelve hours or overnight in cold water, changing water at least once. Drain. Bring cod to a simmer in cold water to cover and simmer 10–15 minutes. Drain cod and flake the meat with your fingers. Parboil parsnips with skins on for 15–40 minutes; drain, cool, and peel. Cut crosswise into ¼-inch slices.

Make a Mornay sauce (a white sauce flavored with cheese) by melting butter in a quart saucepan. Gently sauté onions and garlic in the butter until they are soft (about 5 minutes). Stir in flour and cook 2 minutes. Heat milk separately and add it all at once to the mixture, stirring vigorously until it smooths out. Add the diced cheese, thyme, and pepper, and taste for seasoning. (Don't add salt because the cod is already salted.) Simmer until sauce is nicely thick and smooth.

Cover the bottom of a baking dish with half the sliced parsnips, then the flaked cod, then the rest of the parsnips.

Pour the cream sauce over the whole. Sprinkle the top with the grated Parmesan. Bake at 350° about 15 minutes, or until top is bubbly and brown.

Serves 6.

Glazed Parsnips

2 pounds parsnips
6 tablespoons butter
1 tablespoon sugar (white or brown)
a few drops lemon juice
salt and pepper to taste

Parboil parsnips with their skins on in a goodly amount of boiling water for 15–40 minutes, depending on size and age. Drain, run the parsnips under cold water, cut off the tops, and slip off the skins. Cut crosswise in thin diagonal slices and sauté quickly in butter and sugar until slices are nicely browned. Add a few drops of lemon juice and taste before adding salt and pepper. You may not need the additional seasoning.

Serves 4.

Penn's Parsnip Pudding

(Penn's pudding calls for currants, nutmeg, sugar, cream, and "an Indeferett quantaty" of egg yolks, but I have substituted sultana raisins for currants and honey for sugar, and have added a little rum for fun.)

    2 pounds parsnips
    4 tablespoons butter, melted
    1/2 cup heavy cream
    2 egg yolks
    3 tablespoons dark honey
    1/4 cup dark rum
    1/4 teaspoon nutmeg
    1/2 cup sultana raisins
    a few drops lemon juice
    powdered cinnamon

Parboil parsnips with skins on for 15-40 minutes, drain, cool, peel, and puree in a food processor or food mill or with a potato masher. Add remaining ingredients, except for the cinnamon, and taste for seasoning. If you like, add a little salt or more lemon juice if the mixture seems too bland. Put in a baking dish and bake in a 350° oven for 10-15 minutes, just long enough to thicken the egg yolks and combine flavors. Sprinkle a little cinnamon on top just before serving.

Serves 4-6.

VENISON FEASTS

"Infinite was the company of very large and fat Deere which there we sawe by thousands," Sir Francis Drake reported of California in 1579. So infinite was the company of fat deer in New England that the Indians kept inland deer pastures to fatten and flavor their game with sweet grasses, berries, and browse. Late every fall an entire tribe would set up camp by these pastures so that the men could hunt and the women prepare meats for their winter feasts. When colonists arrived with their cattle, the Indians did not abandon venison for bully beef but, rather, complained that "the white people's cattle eat up all the grass and make the deer scarce."

Colonists, on the other hand, long excluded from the privileges of the chase in their own country, were delighted to be able to hunt deer at will. Since in England venison was the mark of royalty and land-owning aristocrats and gentry, venison had a social cachet superior to beef. A haunch of venison was a mark of status on colonial tables and remained so far into the nineteenth century. America's cookbook writers repeated almost verbatim England's favorite method of spit-roasting a haunch of venison by wrapping it in dough and buttered paper. Thus Sarah Josepha Hale, in *The Ladies' New Book of Cookery* (1852), repeats two centuries later the recipe of Rebecca Price from *The Compleat Cook* (1681), which begins, "Spitt your venison and make some paste with flower and water and role it out very thin and lay it on a sheet of whitebrown paper redy buttered."

It's still a good way to roast venison for your winter table, since you can put the roast in the oven and leave it. Wrapping the meat in dough keeps it moist without larding or basting. Because venison is a lean meat (external fat quickly becomes rancid and should be removed), enclosing the meat in dough, a Dutch oven, or a clay cooker helps to keep in the juices and flavor.

I depend on the kindness of hunter friends for venison, so I never know whether the hunk of frozen meat I am handed is tough or tender. Often the hunter doesn't know either, since a fat old buck may be tenderer than a dry doe. Most cookbooks still prescribe lengthy marination to tenderize tough meat, but I was happy to find Angus Cameron, in *The L. L. Bean Game and Fish Cookbook* (1983), warning hunter-cooks that marinades are better for flavoring than for tenderizing. Today the best way to tenderize venison is to quick-freeze it, a method that replaces both hanging and marinating the meat. Then choose a cooking method appropriate to the cut of meat.

With venison, think beef. Save the loin or tenderloin for roasts and steaks, to be seared quickly and eaten rare (125° on a meat thermometer). Rumps or legs are best braised, with or without liquid, as in a pot roast or dough-wrapped roast. Shoulder, neck, shank, and other trimmings can be finely chopped for stews and meat pies or ground to make sausages, hamburgers, chili, meat loaf, picadillo—all of which take on new flavor with the gamier meat. If you have a home food dryer, you can make delicious venison jerky and pemmican. If you have a smoker, you can inject extra flavor by cold-smoking your sausages or roasts after cooking them.

If you are a lucky hunter whose freezer is bursting with deer, you can vary a diet of venison with different sauces. Instead of the traditional sweet-sour game sauce (used here with Roast Venison in a Paste), you can experiment with a garlic-chili sauce (used here with Roast Loin). With leftover venison, you can improvise venison hash or venison mincemeat for holiday pies. Here I've adapted a rich mincemeat from Marjorie Mosser's *Good Maine Food* (1947). The recipe comes from Kenneth Roberts's grandma and from his childhood memories of helping himself to cupfuls of the stuff whenever the cupboard door was carelessly left unlocked.

If buffalo no longer roam where the deer and the antelope play, at least the company of deer, if not infinite, is more than sufficient to gladden our winter feasts as it once did our ancestors' in the wilderness they called home.

Roast Venison in a Paste

One 6–8-pound roast (haunch or leg) venison
salt and pepper to taste
2 large sheets of parchment paper or foil, plus string
3–4 cups flour
⅓ cup butter or beef drippings, melted
¼ cup vegetable oil

Season the roast with salt and pepper. Place one sheet of the paper over two long pieces of string, with which you'll tie the roast. Make a paste of the flour by adding just enough water to make a dough that you can roll out about ½-inch thick. Roll out the paste in a rectangle big enough to enclose the roast and place it on top of the paper. Cover it with the second sheet of paper. Place the roast on the paper and pour the butter or beef drippings over the meat to coat it on all sides.
Enclose the roast in the paper and paste

and tie the bundle tightly. Coat the outside paper with oil to prevent burning (not necessary with foil), and place on a rack in a roasting pan. Pour ½-inch of boiling water in the bottom of the pan. Bake at 350° for about 20–25 minutes per pound. Remove paper and paste, baste the meat with a little extra butter, dust it with flour, and return it to the oven to brown slightly, 10–15 minutes. Remove roast to a serving platter while you make the Currant-Cranberry Sauce.

Serves 4–6.

Currant-Cranberry Sauce

1 cup beef stock
1 cup port wine
¼ cup cranberries
¼ cup currant jelly
2 tablespoons lemon juice

Put all the ingredients in a blender and puree. Add the puree to the roasting pan and scrape up all the meat juices. Adjust sweet and sour by adding more jelly or lemon juice.

Yields about 2½ cups sauce.

Roast Venison Loin with Garlic-Chili

1 large or 2 small venison loin roasts
½ cup olive oil
4 cloves garlic, crushed
1 dried chili pod, seeds removed
½ cup each chopped onions, carrots, and celery

1 cup red wine
2 cups beef stock
¼ cup bourbon
¼ teaspoon each ground cumin and oregano
salt and pepper to taste
2-3 tablespoons butter

Roll the loin in half the olive oil to coat on all sides
and roast at 450° for 15-35 minutes, depending on size
(meat is rare at 125° on a meat thermometer). Baste
frequently with oil as needed. In ¼ cup of the oil, sauté
the garlic, chili, and vegetables about 5 minutes. Add
wine and pour the mixture into a blender to puree it.
Return puree to saucepan, add stock, bourbon, and seasonings, and simmer 10-15 minutes. When roast is done,
remove it to a serving platter and pour the sauce into the
roasting pan to scrape up meat juices. Swirl in butter and
pour sauce over the roast.

Serves 4-8.

Venison Sausage

2½ pounds venison trimmings
1 pound fat and lean pork
1 clove garlic, minced
1½ teaspoons salt
1 teaspoon black pepper
1½ teaspoons pure ground chili
½ teaspoon each sage, thyme, and oregano
¼ teaspoon cayenne pepper, or to taste
2-3 tablespoons red wine

Grind meats coarsely in a food grinder or
processor. (If you use a processor, freeze

meat half an hour before chopping.) Mix in remaining ingredients and shape meat into patties or stuff into pork casings.

Serves 4-6.

Grandma's Venison Mincemeat

3 cups finely chopped cooked venison
1 cup finely chopped beef suet
6 cups peeled, cored, and chopped apples
1 cup each raisins and currants
½ cup each finely chopped citron
    and candied orange peel
2 cups brown sugar
½ cup molasses
¼ cup each lemon juice and cider vinegar
1 teaspoon salt
½ teaspoon each cinnamon, nutmeg,
    and ginger
¼ teaspoon cloves
½-1 cup brandy

Simmer all ingredients together, except for the spices and brandy, for about 2 hours. Remove from heat and stir in remaining ingredients to taste. Spoon into hot, clean jars, seal, and keep in a cold room or refrigerator. If possible, make two weeks ahead to let mixture ripen.

Yields enough for four 8-9-inch pies.

THE REDSKINNED
CRANBERRY

The Wampanoags of Cape Cod called it "bitter berry," the English "bounce berry," and the Dutch "crane berry." Each named a different quality of the tart, sturdy, bog berry that grows wild where native cranes and herons tread, and that we now cultivate as cranberries. For the Wampanoags and other New England tribes, the wild cranberry was nearly as useful as corn. Its acid pulp and strong skin gave the berry, dried or frozen, a good shelf life. Indians pounded the berry into dried meat and fat to make the traveling snacks they called pemmican. They sweetened the berry with maple sap to enliven their breakfast cereal and their birch-pot roasts and stews. They ground the berry to make a poultice for poisoned-arrow wounds and a dye to redden both human and animal skins.

The Indians taught the colonists how to make "a delicate Sauce" of cranberries boiled with maple sap to put on meats. John Josselyn noted in 1672 that this was good "especially for roasted mutton."

Colonists also found cranberries a good substitute for gooseberries or sour cherries in their English tarts. Sailors in the nineteenth century were grateful for the berries' medicinal powers: they put cranberries in their gruel to prevent scurvy, just as they put limes in their rum. Landlubbers, too, found the berries efficacious for health.

Mrs. N. M. K. Lee, of *The Cook's Own Book* (1832), advised Boston housekeepers that "the juice makes a fine drink for people in fevers."

A berry that thrived in waste places and grew better in sand than in earth became a profitable commercial crop as early as 1816 for Henry Hall, of Dennis on Cape Cod. Throughout the nineteenth century, New Englanders transplanted cranberry cuttings to other bogs—in the Pine Barrens of New Jersey, the marshes of Wisconsin, and the wetlands of the Oregon coast. The berry's thick skin enabled harvesters to use first wooden scoops with rakelike teeth and then power-driven pickers. Today, harvesters use eggbeater machines that stir up the flooded fields so that the loosened berries will float to the top of the water. The bog men then "corral" the berries into great floating wheels of scarlet, "rafting" them to shore to load into trucks for the processing plant. To separate good berries from bad, each berry must bounce on a conveyor belt before it is processed into juice or sauce.

Unfortunately, the very ubiquity of bottled cranberry juice and canned sauce has caused us to neglect this assertive and flashy fruit, except as a relish on the Thanksgiving table or as a decoration on the Christmas tree. Also, commercial cranberry products are usually too strong and too sweet. With cranberries, as with many showy things, less is more. If we think of the cranberry as a miniature red lemon, we may recover old uses and discover new ones.

I have made pemmican in a processor by grinding dried cranberries with homemade beef jerky, beef suet, and butter, and have found the mixture to be delicious but not, perhaps, for everyone. Another Indian use of the berry, however, in a succotash of fresh corn and beans, *is* for everyone who likes a sharp acid bite and bright red beads of color for contrast. A Germanic use of the berry, in Wisconsin, is in a cold tart soup, where cranberries can

substitute for sour cherries to make a cinnamon- and clove-spiced broth soothed with cream.

Our traditional cranberry relish or sauce for turkey can be extended to use with all kinds of meat and fowl— pork, venison, duck. Cranberries have an affinity for the sweet acid of oranges, and I combine the two constantly: in a raw relish with fresh pineapple and walnuts or in a sauce of whole cranberries baked in orange juice. The sauce can then be turned into a sweeter and sourer game sauce with port and vinegar; into a scarlet puree to top a rich and crunchy almond cheesecake; into a frozen ice or granité as refreshing as it is colorful; and into a white wine spritzer that leans toward a kir.

Instead of using lemon to accent your soups, meats, tarts, and sherbets, think cranberry. It's not a bad way to pay tribute to those bouncing bog berries that, for centuries before the white man came, delighted the red man with their red and bitter fruit.

Cranberry Succotash

4 tablespoons butter
2 green onions, tops included, chopped
1/4 cup raw cranberries
1 1/2 cups lima beans, cooked
2 cups raw corn kernels
salt and pepper to taste

Melt butter in a large skillet, add the onions and cranberries, and sauté 2–3 minutes. Add the cooked beans and raw corn, season, and continue cooking for another 3 minutes to mix flavors and cook the corn.

Serves 4.

Cold Cranberry Soup

¼ cup minced onions
1⅓ cups raw cranberries
4 cups chicken broth
¼ cup red wine
2 teaspoons sugar, or to taste
½ teaspoon black pepper
¼ teaspoon each of cinnamon and cloves
½ cup fresh orange juice
¼ cup heavy cream

Add the onions and cranberries to the chicken broth, with the wine and seasonings, and bring to a simmer. Cook 4-5 minutes, or until the skins of the berries have burst. Puree the mixture in a blender with the orange juice. Add heavy cream and taste for sweetness and sourness. Chill thoroughly until ready to serve.

Serves 4-6.

Cran-Pineapple Relish

1 pound cranberries
1 fresh pineapple, cubed
pulp and rind of 1 orange
¾-1 cup superfine sugar
1 cup chopped walnuts

Put all but the nuts in a food processor or blender and chop coarsely. Add chopped nuts. Chill before serving.

Yields about 6 cups.

Cranberry-Orange Sauce

2 cups cranberries
1 cup fresh orange juice
1/2–3/4 cup sugar

Bake the cranberries with the juice and sugar at 325°
for about 20 minutes, or until the skins have burst. Leave
berries whole or puree them in a processor or blender.
Yields about 3 cups.

Cranberry Game Sauce

1/4 cup Cranberry-Orange Sauce, pureed
juice and rind of 1 orange
1/2 cup meat broth
1/3 cup port
1 tablespoon red wine vinegar
1/2 teaspoon black pepper
1/8 teaspoon red pepper
2 tablespoons butter

Blend all the ingredients except the butter in a saucepan. Bring to a simmer and taste for sweetness and sourness. Add butter just before serving to smooth out the
sauce.
Yields about 1½ cups.

Cran-Nut Cheesecake

1½ cups blanched almonds
2 pounds cream cheese
1⅓ cups sugar
4 eggs
1 teaspoon vanilla extract
½ teaspoon almond extract
2–3 tablespoons butter
½ cup zweiback or gingersnap crumbs
1½ cups Cranberry-Orange Sauce, pureed

Toast almonds on a baking sheet for 10 minutes in a 325° oven. Chop them coarsely in a food processor or by hand. Beat the cheese with the sugar and eggs until fluffy. Add vanilla and almond extract and fold in the nuts. Butter the bottom and sides of a springform pan and sprinkle with crumbs. Pour in the cheese mixture. Bake at 350° for 30 minutes. Spread top with the cranberry puree and bake 30 minutes more, or until cheese is firm but not dry. Cool before removing cake from pan.
Serves 8.

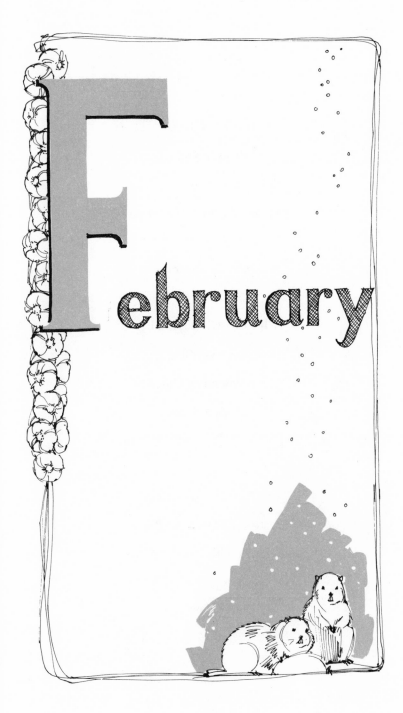

February

February

OUR GARLIC REVOLUTION

Garlic Soup

Garlic Mayonnaise (*Aioli*)

Garlic Fish Stew (*Bourride*)

Garlic Cod (*Brandade de Morue*)

Veal *Gremolata*

FRUITS OF THE SEA

Scalloped Clams

Hangtown-Fry Omelet

Boston Scrod

Cod with Oyster-Anchovy Sauce

COOKING IN CLAY

Buttermilk-Oatmeal Bread

Braised Duck with Leeks and Orange

Chicken with Oysters

Clay-Baked Fish

OUR GARLIC REVOLUTION

One of the most permeating of America's many revolutions in the 1960s was the garlic revolution. I can remember the dark years of the 1940s, when garlic was thought to be subversive of the American way of life and only the daring risked more than a quick rub of the salad bowl with a cut garlic clove. Back then, to eat a loaf of garlic bread was an act of bravado and to eat a garlic-laden spaghetti sauce was an act of liberation.

In the 1950s, however, Elizabeth David established a beachhead in England by publishing, in her *Mediterranean Cooking*, no less than a garlic manifesto. In the 1960s, James Beard and Julia Child mounted a two-pronged attack on the American heartland. So complete was their triumph that by the 1970s California's culinary bolshies, headed by Alice Waters, were roasting whole heads of garlic at Chez Panisse and were staging all-garlic dinners, which began with garlic soup and ended with garlic sorbet.

In the 1980s Americans have at last discovered the wisdom of ancient Egypt, Greece, and Rome: that garlic is not only one of the world's tastiest foods, but is actually good for you. Any European herbal will list garlic as a tonic and a stimulant—to aid digestion, prevent liver trouble, and defeat hypertension. French herbals will also list garlic as an aphrodisiac. I've often wondered whether Colette, who lay abed chewing garlic cloves the way Americans chew gum, was improving her health or her amatory prowess.

I joined the garlic revolution with my first bowl of garlic soup, which I made from Elizabeth David's recipe, despite my fear that she was spouting nonsense when she assured us that with garlic, *more* is less. A whole head of garlic in a pot of broth, she claimed (as Beard would do later with his Forty-Garlic Chicken), lessened rather than increased the taste of garlic. Garlic in quantity proved to be not only mild in taste but as nourishing and filling as protein. With a poached egg on top, garlic soup can be a three-course meal.

After a summer in Provence, I became such a seasoned garlic trouper that I could take in stride that pungent combination of garlic and olive oil the locals call *aioli* (the French for garlic is *ail*). *Aioli* spells Provence the way sunflowers spell Van Gogh, and I learned to spoon garlic mayonnaise on everything from fresh vegetables to eggs, shrimp, cod, boiled potatoes, and chicken salads.

Best of all, I learned to thicken fish broth with *aioli* to make the triumphant fish stew of Provence called *bourride*. As traditional as *bouillabaisse*, a good *bourride* is much easier to make, particularly now that the food processor makes short work of what was once done laboriously by mortar, pestle, and whisk. You can make a frothy and creamy *bourride* in seconds. The processor also makes quick work of an incredibly rich and delicious dish traditional to fish Fridays in Provence. It is *brandade de morue*, and in it salt cod is turned into a kind of garlic mayonnaise with olive oil and heavy cream to make a stiff puree as smooth as butter.

On a recent trip to Italy, I rediscovered a fine Italian use of garlic in the garnish they call *gremolata*, in which garlic is minced with parsley and lemon and sprinkled on a simple stew such as *ossobuco*, braised veal shanks. The chopped lemon pulp and rind cut the garlic and enliven the parsley in a way that complements foods such as poached chicken or fish or, as I've used it here, veal sautéed as scallopini.

Needless to say, *fresh* garlic is essential. Throw away any dried, withered, or sprouting cloves. Throw away also that old garlic press we all bought in the 1960s in the first flush of garlic enthusiasm. A press reduces the sweetest clove to fiber and liquid. Instead, take a heavy knife like a cleaver, place your unpeeled cloves on a chopping board, and mash them with the side of the knife. You can then easily remove the peel and mince the cloves. To remove the garlic smell from fingers and board, rub them with half a lemon.

Today most of America's garlic is grown in Gilroy, California, which stages an annual garlic festival that rivals the renowned festival of Marseilles, where garlic braids and wreaths hang from every roof. Garlic, it seems, has forged another link in the ancient Franco-American alliance that links the "Marseillaise" to the "Star Spangled Banner" and the chicken salads of the Fourth of July to the *bourrides* of Bastille Day.

Garlic Soup

1 whole head garlic
6 cups chicken broth
1 medium onion, chopped
1 tablespoon each butter and olive oil
pinch of saffron
salt and pepper to taste
4 large slices French bread, toasted
4 poached eggs

Separate the cloves of garlic and put them, unpeeled, into a saucepan with the chicken broth. Cover tightly and simmer 1 hour. Strain the broth into another pot and slip off the garlic skins when they are cool enough to handle. Sauté the onion in the butter, oil, and seasonings until soft. Put the garlic, onion, and 2 or 3 cups of the broth into a blender, process until smooth, and combine with the rest of the broth. Heat briefly to blend flavors. When ready to serve, float a slice of toast and a poached egg on top of each bowl of soup.

Serves 4.

Garlic Mayonnaise
(Aioli)

4 large cloves garlic, mashed and peeled
1 teaspoon Dijon mustard
1/4–1/2 teaspoon salt
1/4 teaspoon white pepper
1 whole egg
1 egg yolk
1/4 cup fresh basil leaves or other herbs
   (optional)
3/4 cup olive oil
lemon juice to taste

Put the garlic cloves with the mustard, salt, pepper, egg, egg yolk, and basil in a blender. Blend a few seconds. While the blender is on, add 1/4 cup of the oil, blend thoroughly, then add remaining oil slowly in a thin, steady stream until the mayonnaise thickens. Add lemon juice to taste.

Yields about 1 cup.

Garlic Fish Stew
(Bourride)

½ cup dry white wine
½ cup half and half
1 cup or more fish broth or clam juice
bay leaf, thyme, salt, and pepper to taste
1 onion, minced
2 pounds white fish fillets, such as flounder,
   haddock, or cod
½-¾ cup Garlic Mayonnaise (*aioli*)

Make a bouillon of the wine, half and half, fish broth, seasonings, and onion. Simmer about 10 minutes in a pan large enough to hold the fish fillets in a single layer when you add them. Add fish and, if needed, more broth or wine to cover the fish. Cover the pan and barely simmer 4-7 minutes, or until fish is just tender. Pour the liquid off into a saucepan. Add a little of the hot liquid to the mayonnaise to thin it, then beat in enough of the remaining liquid with a wire whisk to make a foamy sauce. Pour the sauce over the fish. Boiled white potatoes make a good accompaniment.
Serves 4-6.

Garlic Cod
(Brandade de Morue)

1 pound salt cod
⅔ cup olive oil
½-1 cup heavy cream
2-3 cloves garlic, peeled
pepper to taste
1 cup mashed potatoes (optional)

Soak cod overnight in cold water to cover. Change water more than once if cod seems very salty and dry. Drain and rinse well. Simmer very gently in fresh water 10-15 minutes, or until cod is soft. Warm the oil and cream in separate pans. Mash the garlic and put it in a food processor. Add the drained cod and process until blended. With the processor running, add half the oil gradually through the lid opening, then half the cream. Repeat and process until puree is smooth. Add pepper and taste for seasoning. If you add potatoes, beat them in by hand.

Serves 6-8.

Veal Gremolata

1 pound veal scallops
salt and pepper to taste
2 tablespoons olive oil
4 tablespoons butter
Garnish: 2 cloves garlic, minced;
   1 small lemon, seeded and diced (rind and all);
   1/2 cup minced parsley

If veal scallops are not very thin, pound them with a meat tenderizer or the rim of a thick plate. Salt and pepper them on both sides. In a heavy frying pan, heat the oil and butter and add the scallops a few at a time so that they will brown quickly, cooking less than a minute on each side. Have the garnish ready. Make it by mixing together the minced garlic, lemon, and parsley. Sprinkle the scallops with the garnish and cover with any remaining pan juices.

Serves 2-4.

FRUITS OF THE SEA

In New England, February is a barren and discouraging month. The putative garden is either a mud hole or an ice pond. In such a month one major comfort is the unending fertility of the sea, when its salt fruits are at their best. The most comforting are the most common because the most fertile. I think of the bisexual oyster and the multitudinous clam and cod.

So plentiful were oysters in nineteenth-century America that Eliza Leslie, in her 1837 *Directions for Cookery*, thought nothing of directing her readers to "Take a hundred and fifty fine large oysters...." Such cookbooks advised creaming, stewing, and scalloping oysters by the barrel load. The East shipped barreled oysters to the Midwest by stagecoach, canal boat, and, finally, locomotive. The West had oysters of their own and had them so abundantly that pioneers barbecued them over campfires and prospectors tossed them into scrambled eggs, which were scarcer than hen's teeth during the Gold Rush, to make a "Hangtown Fry." Despite the depletion today of our native beds, America still shucks oysters by the bushel and sells them by the pound—currently, some 50 million pounds a year.

Clams were so plentiful that they were a mainstay for the Indian tribes of New England, as witnessed by the acres of shell heaps still found along bays and beaches from Connecticut to Maine. Many clam banks were three feet deep and twenty acres wide. Cod was once so plentiful that the body of the cod was thought vulgar in comparison to its head and shoulders, a delicacy which was roasted and carved. Old-time Atlantic fishermen will still tell you that the cod's cheeks and "tongues," meaning its throat muscles, are its best parts, although "sounds," or air bladders along the spine, are also much favored.

In each of my recipes here, I've updated a traditional oyster, clam, or cod dish with current flavorings or methods. I've scalloped clams by the same method as oysters, with lots of buttery crumbs to protect their tender flesh. Eliza Leslie used giant clam shells to bake her "scolloped" oysters or clams, when she placed them over the coals and browned their crumbed tops with a red-hot shovel. For a "Hangtown Fry" I've browned oysters in cracker crumbs and rolled them in an omelet to make a meal as hefty as a prospector's hunger for gold in Hangtown, California, where the dish presumably originated.

I've failed to wangle cod's cheeks, tongues, or sounds from my local fishmonger, but cod steaks or fillets are readily available. Although "scrod" properly refers to a codling, or young cod, today the name has become as generic as "cod," and it refers to any number of related deep-water fish such as haddock and hake. But whatever scrod defines in substance, it sounds like Boston. A proper Bostonian might raise an eyebrow at the Worcestershire and vermouth I've added to a simple baked scrod, but Boston is no longer the simple domain of the Lowells, the Cabots, and God.

Miss Leslie of Philadelphia had no puritanical qualms about dressing up a cod for the dinner table. She garnished a whole cod with its roe and liver and served it with oyster sauce in a boat. "Or you may make a sauce," she suggested, "by flavouring your melted butter with a glass

of port wine, and an anchovy boned and minced." With these tips from Eliza, I've baked or "poached" cod steaks in foil, or parchment paper if you prefer, topped with an oyster-anchovy sauce that delicately flavors the cod.

In winter months like February, no pleasure is too small. In eating the common oyster, clam, and cod, we can commune with numberless generations of Americans who have found comfort and pleasure in the harvest of our waters, from sea to shining sea.

Scalloped Clams

> 4 cups shucked clams, about 4 dozen if
>   cherrystone size
> ¼ pound (1 stick) butter
> ¼ cup minced green onions
> 2 cups fresh bread crumbs (4-6 slices bread)
> ¼ cup minced parsley
> ¼ teaspoon mace
> salt and black and cayenne pepper to taste
> juice of ½ lemon

If clams are cherrystone size or smaller, leave whole; if larger, chop coarsely. Melt butter and sauté onions about 2 minutes to soften them. Add bread crumbs (make these from white bread slices, crusts removed, chopped in a food processor), parsley, and seasonings and mix well. Spread half the crumbs in a baking dish large enough to hold the clams in a single layer, or use large scallop shells. Cover the crumbs with the clams and sprinkle them with lemon juice. Cover with remaining crumbs and bake at 450° for 5-8 minutes, or until top is browned.

Serves 4.

Hangtown-Fry Omelet

4 medium oysters, shucked
salt and pepper to taste
3 large eggs, beaten
½ cup cracker crumbs
3 tablespoons butter
2 strips cooked bacon (to garnish)

Season oysters with salt and pepper, dip them into the beaten eggs, roll them in cracker crumbs, and sauté them quickly on both sides in 2 tablespoons of the butter until lightly browned (1-2 minutes on each side). Melt remaining butter in an omelet pan and when butter begins to bubble, pour in the remaining beaten egg. As soon as the bottom of the eggs begins to set (10-15 seconds), add the oysters and roll up the omelet with the oysters inside. Garnish with the strips of bacon.
Serves 1.

Boston Scrod

2 pounds scrod fillets, about 1 inch thick
1 cup milk
1 tablespoon lemon juice
1 teaspoon Worcestershire sauce
½ cup vermouth or white wine
4 tablespoons butter
salt and pepper to taste

Marinate the scrod in a covered bowl or plastic bag with the milk, lemon juice, and Worcestershire sauce for at least an hour. Drain. Place fillets in a buttered baking dish with vermouth, butter, and seasonings, cover tightly, and bake at 400° about 10 minutes (a rule of thumb is to cook fish 10 minutes per inch of thickness).

Serves 4.

Cod with Oyster-Anchovy Sauce

2 pounds cod fillets or 4 cod steaks
salt and black and cayenne pepper to taste
3 tablespoons olive oil
6 tablespoons butter
1 medium onion, chopped fine
1 clove garlic, minced
4 anchovy fillets, mashed
1 pint shucked oysters
fresh parsley or thyme

Season the cod well on both sides, cover it, and let it sit 30 minutes or more to let the seasonings take effect. Prepare 1 large sheet of foil, or 4 smaller ones, to make packets for baking the fish in one layer. Put a few drops of olive oil in the center of each piece of foil. In remaining oil and butter, sauté the onion, garlic, and mashed anchovies about 5 minutes. Remove from heat and add the oysters with their liquid. Center the cod on each sheet of foil and cover the fish with the oyster sauce. Sprinkle the top with a little minced parsley or fresh thyme. Pull the foil up around the cod and make a seam lengthwise at the top, leaving a pocket of air between the fish and the seam so that the fish will steam as well as bake. Bake at 400° for about 10 minutes if the fish is an inch thick. Serve fish in the opened foil.

Serves 4.

COOKING IN CLAY

Four centuries ago, when English settlers began to set up housekeeping in New England, they were dismayed to discover that they had left the Iron Age for the Stone Age. The British had known iron since 400 B.C., but in America they found aborigines still baking food in wet clay in the ashes of their campfires or in stone-lined pits where the earth itself served as an oven. Francis Higginson of Salem, Massachusetts, warned fellow settlers in 1630 to bring with them a year's provisions and the pots to cook them in. His "Catalogue of Such Needful Things" included "1 iron pot, 1 Kettel, 1 Frying Pan, 1 Gridiron, 2 Skellets, 1 spit."

Yet even in England, West Country folk continued to use until this century the small beehive clay ovens of their ancestors. In the seventeenth and eighteenth centuries, they exported many of these ovens to America. A nineteenth-century historian of New Hampshire describes how early settlers there built "Dutch" ovens, as they were called, "of stone and clay, out doors, on the top of a great stump cut evenly for the purpose, and in it the housewife baked bread, cakes, pies, beef, geese, turkeys, chicken-pies so appetizing, and pork and beans."

While the earthenware bean pot continued to get good use, the all-purpose clay oven was eventually replaced by the iron Dutch oven, by the cast-iron stove and—finally—by gas, electric, and microwave ovens. Good potteries like the Bennington Potters in Vermont developed glazed clay cookers early on, but unglazed cookers were so little known in this country that even today they are best known by their German name, *Schlemmertopf.* Because it is unglazed, this low-fired clay pot is first soaked in cold water and is then placed in a cold oven. The heat is then turned high to simulate earlier methods of cooking in wet clay, methods that steam as well as bake the food within the pot.

As a child of my time, captive to the iron, aluminum, and now Calphalon age, I find cooking in fired or unfired clay as venturesome as an aborigine might find using an electric plug. I have also found that clay can do some things better than iron. I learned from the Indians of the Southwest, whose adobe ovens resemble those of ancient Egypt and Rome, the virtues of baking bread in clay. Clay retains and distributes heat evenly, long after the heat source has been removed. The result is a beautifully crusted bread.

To bake bread in clay, you can use a large wet flowerpot, seasoned well by a coating of oil inside and out and baked empty in a hot oven. You let the dough rise in the pot and then invert the pot on a greased tile or baking sheet in a hot oven so that the pot forms a mini-oven within the bigger one.

Clay cooking is also unbeatable for long, slow cooking that mingles flavors while sealing in the juices of fowl, meat, or fish. Clay cookers developed wherever winters were long and cold and the heat source steady. From the northern Chinese I've adapted a delicious braised duck flavored with leeks and orange, as suggested by Karen Lee in her 1983 *Chinese Cooking Secrets* and her mentor Grace Chu. From the 1886 *Kansas Home Cook-Book,* I've adapted a recipe for oyster-stuffed chicken to cook with vegetables in a clay cooker.

I've recently come upon a line of handsome stoneware cookers made by the sculptor Montgomery

Smith of Swan Island Designs in Richmond, Maine. Although his terra-cotta is unglazed, it is fired at high temperatures to make it nonporous and nonsticking, so you can use it as you would any glazed earthenware casserole, without soaking or starting it in a cold oven. In his straight-sided cookers you can bake bread as well as braise meats and vegetables.

To get back to the real primal stuff, however, I decided to bake a fish by enclosing it in raw terra-cotta clay, which I had to buy in a twenty-five-pound hunk from my local art supply store. The fun part was sculpting a fish with scales, fins, a bulging eye, and an open mouth, and presenting my baked artwork with a flourish before I broke it open with a hammer to the astonishment and apprehension of my guests. To everyone's relief, including my own, the fish inside was herb-scented, moist, and tender. But with all that leftover clay, I had to invite my younger neighbors in for a session of mud pies. Were I colonizing some new land today, my own Catalogue of Such Needful Things might include one clay cooker, but not twenty-five pounds of uncooked clay.

Buttermilk-Oatmeal Bread

¾–1 cup steel-cut oats
¼ cup boiling water
1 package dry yeast
½ cup warm water (110–115°)
5–6 cups unbleached flour
1 tablespoon salt
1¼ cups buttermilk

Pour the boiling water over the oats and soak for 20 minutes. Dissolve yeast in the warm water.

Add 5 cups of the flour to the salt, buttermilk, oats, and yeast and mix well. Add more flour if necessary. Knead dough well and put it to rise until doubled in a well-greased clay cooker or flowerpot. Punch dough down, let rise again, and cover the cooker or pot with a clay lid (or inverted flowerpot) to bake at 400° for 30–40 minutes, or until crust sounds hollow when tapped.

Yields 1 large loaf.

Braised Duck with Leeks and Orange

One 4-pound duck (with giblets)
8 slices fresh ginger root

STUFFING:
duck giblets
½ cup cooked rice
¼ cup minced parsley
1 clove garlic, minced
salt and black and red pepper to taste

2 leeks
rind and juice of 1 orange
⅓ cup duck or chicken stock
3 tablespoons soy sauce
⅓ cup dry sherry
½ teaspoon Chinese five-spice powder
1 tablespoon honey

Remove excess fat from duck (inside cavity and under the skin between breast and thigh). Slip the ginger slices under the breast skin. Prick duck skin all over with a fork and roast on a rack in a pan at 400° for 40 minutes to cook out the fat. (Place duck breast down for the first 20 minutes and breast up for the remaining 20.) Cook gizzard and heart in a little broth and mince them. Cut up the raw duck liver, add to other giblets and mix into the rice, parsley, garlic, and seasonings for the stuffing. Spoon stuffing into the duck cavity.

Cut off roots of the leeks, wash the leaves well, and cut the leeks in slivers 3″ long by 1/4″ wide. Place leeks in a layer in a cooker and put the duck, breast up, on top. Mix orange juice, stock, soy sauce, sherry, and spice powder and pour over the duck. Dribble honey over the breast and sprinkle with grated orange rind. Cover and bake at 350° for 1-1½ hours, or until meat is chopstick tender. Remove duck to carve.

Serves 2-4.

Chicken with Oysters

One 4-pound roasting chicken
1 pint shucked oysters, drained
1/4 cup minced parsley
4 tablespoons butter, softened
2 onions and 2 carrots, diced
3 new potatoes, diced
salt, pepper, and thyme

Stuff the cavity of the chicken with oysters and parsley. Spread butter over the top of the bird and surround it with the vegetables. Season and bake at 350° for 1½ hours.

Serves 4.

Clay-Baked Fish

One 2- to 4-pound firm-fleshed whole fish
    (pompano, trout, bass, bluefish)
fresh herbs, such as tarragon, thyme, mint
salt and pepper to taste
8–10 pounds terra-cotta clay
4–6 tablespoons butter, softened
1 tablespoon tarragon vinegar
2–3 tablespoons fresh tarragon leaves, chopped

Gut fish, leaving head and tail on. Stuff cavity with herbs, salt and pepper fish on both sides, and wrap it entirely in heavy foil. Cover foil on both sides with daubs of clay smoothed together to make a layer ½-inch thick. Sculpt a fish tail, a head with clay eye and mouth, and fish scales (to make scales, stick on thin petals of clay, beginning at the tail and working toward the head). Bake fish at 400° about 40 minutes for 2 pounds (50 minutes for 3 pounds, 60 minutes for 4 pounds). Present fish, then break clay open with a hammer and remove the fish. Carve it into fillets, top and bottom. Cover with a sauce of softened butter whipped with vinegar and tarragon leaves.
    Serves 2–4.

March

March

THOSE BOSSY BEETS

Beet and Orange Soup

Beet and Pink Grapefruit Salad

Cranberry Beets

Hot Beet and Apple Salad

Three-Root Puree

HOMINY GRITS

Breakfast Grits

Hominy Puff

Hominy Stir-Fry

Mexican Hominy with Roasted Peppers

Hominy with Fried Parsley

MARMALADE, BRITISH AND YANK

True Brit Marmalade

Red Pepper Marmalade

Citrus Marmalade

Marmalade Carrot Cake

THOSE BOSSY BEETS

Pity the poor beet. Its virtues have undone it. Lizzie
Kander says it all in her 1930 edition of *The Settlement
Cook Book* when she advises the cook to pickle the old
beets and can the young ones. At harvest time the beet
was too common, too reliable, and too durable to use
fresh. Besides, it was a bleeder. Even Jane Grigson, in
her *Vegetable Book* (1978), admits a personal hostility to
beets: "With all that purple juice bleeding out at the
tiniest opportunity, a cook may reasonably feel that beet-
root has taken over the kitchen and is far too bossy a
vegetable." Best to tame the purploid bully with strong
vinegar or tin cans.

Until the nineteenth century, of course, the vegetables
most often grown were those that were the best for storing
—by drying, pickling, or preserving in the root cellar. In
The Vegetable Garden of 1885, Messieurs Vilmorin and
Andrieux advise the gardener to dig up his beetroots by
the end of October, build them into "pyramidal-shaped
clumps," and cover them with straw and earth for the
winter. A root that preserved intact its firm texture and
extraordinary sweetness was invaluable as winter food
for man and beast, but the fact that cows liked beets
did not improve their status on the table.

In Russia, the word "borscht" (which now means
any kind of soup with beets in it) originally meant
"cow parsnips." For mainstream America, beets became

associated with poverty, with food for cows, peasants, and Slavic-Jewish immigrants, whose addiction to beet soups turned the Catskills into the "Borscht Belt." Lizzie Kander preserves the strength of this tradition in her recipes for two kinds of "Russian-style" borscht: "Milchik," made with a base of milk, and "Fleischik," made with a meat base. She also includes a number of excellent pickle recipes, from a bossy "Beet and Horseradish Relish" to a sophisticated "Beet Preserves" made with lemons, almonds, and fresh ginger root.

Unfortunately, New England generally followed the English tradition of taming beets in a sweet-sour sauce thickened by flour or cornstarch. In 1896 Fannie Farmer tried to upgrade the dish by giving it an Ivy League name, "Harvard Beets." Yalies, not to be outdone, substituted flour and butter for cornstarch, and orange juice for vinegar, to produce "Yale Beets."

Only recently have we begun to look anew at garden-fresh beets and, with the help of fashionable gardener-chefs like Alice Waters of Chez Panisse, to grow beets the size of Ping-Pong balls instead of baseballs. The best cache of beet recipes that I know is provided by Southerners Stringfellow Barr and Stella Standard in *The Kitchen Garden Book* (1956). They give us such lovelies as "Beets and Sour Cherry Soup," "Beets in Pomegranate Sauce," and "Beet Soufflé."

Cooking beets is best done by either boiling or baking them unpeeled with at least 2 inches of stems left on to avoid excess bleeding. Baby beets are best flavored only with butter and a little lemon or orange for tartness. Citrus of any kind has an affinity with the beet because the tartness cuts the sweetness.

Here I've added citrus to a beet soup, salad, and sauce. I've adapted a clear beet and orange-juice soup from *The Kitchen Garden Book* and flavored it with fresh coriander. I've made a salad of beets, pink grapefruit (instead of the usual orange), and red onions, served on beet greens and accented with walnuts. And I've made a sauce of orange juice, cranberries, and honey for a sweet-sour puree free of cornstarch.

Another classic use of beets is in a Waldorf salad, which I've varied here in the Dutch way to make a hot salad of beets, apples, onions, horseradish, and fresh ginger root, soothed with sour cream. It's the kind of salad that goes well with pickled or salted herring. Finally, I've returned to the root world to make a puree of beets, potatoes, and celery roots (or knobs). The idea of mashing boiled potatoes with beets roasted in ashes comes from *The Buckeye Cookbook*, printed in Minneapolis in 1883. "This is a New England dish," the *Buckeye* claims, "and very delicious for harvest time, when beets are young and sweet." Too young and sweet to be bossy, or maybe just so young and sweet you don't care.

Beet and Orange Soup

1 pound beets with tops
5 cups chicken stock
2 teaspoons red wine vinegar
½ teaspoon ground coriander
salt and pepper to taste
1 cup fresh orange juice
Garnish: orange slices and fresh coriander sprigs

Scrub unpeeled beets well. Cut off the tops, chop them, and put them in a large saucepan. Shred the beets in a food processor or on a grater. Add them to the pan and cover with the chicken stock. Bring

to a boil, cover, and simmer 25 minutes. Strain the broth and discard the pulp. Add to the broth the vinegar, seasonings, and orange juice. To serve hot, reheat just enough to warm the orange juice. To serve cold, chill well in the refrigerator. Garnish each soup bowl with a slice of orange and a sprig of fresh coriander.

Serves 4.

Beet and Pink Grapefruit Salad

1½ pounds young beets with tops
1 pink grapefruit, peeled and sectioned
½ red Bermuda onion, sliced thin
½ cup chopped walnuts
½ cup olive oil
1 tablespoon walnut oil
¼ cup fruit vinegar
salt and pepper to taste

Scrub beets and cut off the tops. Boil them in water to cover or bake at 350° in a tightly covered dish for 25-60 minutes, depending on beet size. Beets are done when the skin wrinkles easily and slips off. Blanch tops 2-3 minutes in the beet water or in water to cover. Drain well and arrange on a serving plate. Peel beets and slice them very thin. Alternate beet slices with grapefruit sections and onion on top of the greens. Sprinkle with the walnuts and pour over them a dressing of the oils, vinegar, and seasonings.

Serves 4-6.

Cranberry Beets

1 cup cranberries
½ cup fresh orange juice
½ teaspoon cinnamon
2 tablespoons honey, or to taste
1 pound cooked beets, peeled and sliced thin

Make a sauce for the beets by boiling the cranberries, covered, in the orange juice and cinnamon until the cranberries burst. Puree the mixture in a blender and add the honey. Simmer the sliced beets in the sauce for 1-2 minutes to mingle flavors.

Serves 4.

Hot Beet and Apple Salad

2 large beets, cooked and peeled
2 tart apples, cored and quartered
1 small onion, chopped fine
2 tablespoons butter
2-3 tablespoons freshly grated horseradish
2 teaspoons grated ginger root
½ cup sour cream
1 teaspoon lemon juice
salt and pepper to taste
2 Belgian endives

Dice the beets and apples. Sauté the onion in butter until soft. Add the beets, apples, horseradish, and ginger and simmer 3-4 minutes to mix flavors.

Blend the sour cream with the lemon juice and seasonings and fold into the beet mixture. Taste and add more
lemon or horseradish if needed. Arrange endive leaves in
a circle on the serving plate and heap the salad mixture
in the center.

Serves 4.

Three-Root Puree

1-2 beets
1 large Idaho potato
1 celery root (knob)
2 tablespoons butter
½ cup yoghurt
salt and pepper to taste

Scrub unpeeled beets and potato and cover with
boiling salted water in a saucepan. Peel celery root and
add to the pan. Cover and boil vegetables 25–40 minutes,
depending on size. Peel beets and potato under cold running water. Put vegetables through a food mill, a ricer, or
the grating disk of a processor. Add butter, yoghurt, and
seasonings and fluff well.

Serves 4.

HOMINY GRITS

Had you lived in deep country 150 years ago, you might have had, in the yard near your kitchen, both a samp mill and an ash hopper. The samp mill was a giant mortar and pestle made from a tree stump and a block of wood. The block was suspended from a tree branch that acted as a spring. You would use this samp mill to crack dried corn and turn the kernels into coarse meal or fine flour. The ash hopper was a V-shaped wooden funnel that held wood ashes. You would run water through the ashes to make lye, which you'd then use to soften the tough outer skins or hulls of whole corn kernels in order to make hominy.

Our colonial ancestors, baffled by the foreignness of corn, which they first called "Guinney or Turkie wheate," had to learn a whole new vocabulary before they could learn from the Indians how to make this obdurate grain edible. Colonists came to use the words "samp" and "hominy" almost interchangeably to mean processed corn, as in this account by an English traveler in 1668: "[They] make a kind of loblolly to eat with Milk, which they call Sampe; they beat [corn] in a Mortar and sift the Flower out of it; the remainder they call Homminey, which they put into a Pot of two or three Gallons, with Water, and boyl it upon a gentle Fire till it be like a Hasty Pudden." A "Hasty Pudden" made of wheat "flower" was the instant cereal of the home country, just as "Sampe" was of the colonies.

If the word "samp" dropped out of modern English,

"hominy" hung on and was sometimes joined by "grits." In most of America "hominy" came to mean lye hominy, or whole kernels that were hulled but not ground. In the South, however, "hominy" came to mean the hulled kernels ground coarsely to make "grits." Grits are called "hominy grits" in most of the South, "but never," says my Charleston friend Elizabeth Hamilton, "*never* in Charleston." In Charleston grits are perversely called "hominy." Yankees will do better to learn the lingo of New Orleans, where the whole kernels are known as "big hominy" and the ground kernels as "small" or "little hominy."

Many Southeasterners will tell you that the only hominy worth eating is small hominy, which they eat for breakfast from the cradle to the grave. They eat grits with everything—butter, gravy, country ham, river shrimp, eggs-cream-and-cheese, fried fish, veal steak, and that very local Charleston specialty, John's Island hot liver pudding.

Southwesterners, on the other hand, will grind small hominy even smaller to make *masa* for tamales and tortillas. But their status corn is big hominy, which Indians and Mexicans dry and call *posole*, and from which they make a festive dish of pork, *posole*, and red peppers. As a Southwestern Californian raised on canned whole hominy, I am still devoted to big hominy despite my conversion to grits. The problem for migrant devotees nowadays, however, is how to get hold of hominy or grits, since supermarket shelves in the North are often devoid of either. Commercial quick or instant grits may be available, and if you're desperate you'll settle.

It is possible to make your own hominy by steaming dried corn with wood ashes or limewater in a pressure cooker, but removing the softened and loosened hulls by hand is tedious work. You can also make your own grits by drying the hulled corn and then grinding it in an electric grain mill or blender. But that is not a task for every day, and if you're a hominy or grits addict, you'll want that earthy fix not only every day but sometimes at every meal.

For breakfast I find that there's nothing like plain hot grits, loaded with butter, pepper, and salt or maybe sugar, cinnamon, and cream. For a fancy breakfast, there's hominy-grits spoon bread, made light as a soufflé with egg whites, which *The Corn Cook Book* of 1918 calls a "Hominy Puff." For lunch I like to flavor hominy with sesame oil and fresh crisp vegetables to make a hominy stir-fry, or I sometimes like to combine the bland white grain of hominy with the bitter green of deep-fried parsley. For dinner I shoot the moon with Hominy with Roasted Peppers, a version of Mexican *posole* with sausage as well as pork, and with sweet and hot peppers.

Today, if you live in the country, you probably have neither samp mill nor ash hopper, no more than you have a Jimmy or Ginny to crack your corn and swat your blue-tailed flies. For compensation, however, you may well have more time in which to explore the astonishing variety of "nasaump" and "rockahominie," as our North-eastern tribes once called the processed corn that gave them, and us, true grit.

Breakfast Grits

2 cups boiling water
1½ cups milk
½ teaspoon salt
pepper to taste
1 cup stone-ground grits
4 tablespoons butter

In a saucepan stir water, milk, and seasonings into the grits and cook over low heat 30 minutes, stirring to keep

the grain from scorching. Add butter and cook 5 minutes
more.

Serves 4.

Hominy Puff

1 cup cooked grits
1 cup white cornmeal
4 tablespoons butter, softened
2 eggs, separated
1½ cups sour milk or cream
1 teaspoon salt
1 tablespoon baking powder

While grits are still warm, mix with the cornmeal,
butter, and egg yolks, then add milk, salt, and baking
powder. Beat egg whites until stiff and fold into the grits.
Spoon mixture into a buttered baking dish and bake at
325° about 30 minutes, or until mixture is set.

Serves 4–6.

Hominy Stir-Fry

2 or 3 green onions
1 sweet red pepper
1 tablespoon each olive oil and sesame oil
1 cup each green beans and snow peas
½ cup sliced radishes
2 cups canned hominy (whole kernels)
salt and pepper to taste

Cut onions in 2-inch lengths and then into narrow
strips, including some of the green. Remove stem and

seeds of the pepper and cut it into narrow strips length-wise. In a wok or large skillet, heat the two oils, add onions, pepper, and green beans and sauté 2-3 minutes. Add snow peas and radishes, then the hominy with its liquid. Salt and pepper to taste. Bring to a boil quickly and serve.

Serves 4-6.

Mexican Hominy with Roasted Peppers

2 onions, chopped
2 cloves garlic, minced
2 tablespoons corn oil
2 pounds meaty pork bones (such as spareribs)
1 teaspoon oregano
12 black peppercorns, crushed
1 cup dried hominy*
   (or 2 cups canned hominy)
1 cup freshly made chili sauce from 3 dried chilis,
   such as Ancho, New Mexican, or Anaheim**
   (or 2 tablespoons pure red chili powder)
1 quart chicken broth
3 sweet red or yellow bell peppers, char-grilled
   or broiled
1 Spanish chorizo or Italian hot sausage
salt to taste

*Specialty Mexican stores in large cities sell both canned hominy and the dried hominy, or *posole*. Or you can order *posole* directly from Casados Farms, P.O. Box 1269, San Juan Pueblo, NM 87566.

**To Make Chili Sauce:* Toast chilies briefly in a dry skillet, then run them under cold water to remove stems and seeds. Cover chilies with boiling water and let sit 30 minutes. Puree in a blender with enough of the chili water to make 1 cup.

In a heavy kettle, sauté onions and garlic in the oil. Add pork, seasonings, and dried hominy. Add chili sauce or dried powder and the broth, cover kettle, and simmer 2 hours. Meanwhile, roast sweet peppers on a grill or under the broiler until charred all over. Put them in a paper bag to steam 5 minutes, then peel, remove seeds, and cut flesh in large squares. When dried hominy is tender, add the sausage and simmer gently 5–10 minutes. (If using canned hominy, add with the sausage.) Add peppers and cook another 10 minutes. Taste for seasoning.
Serves 6–8.

Hominy with Fried Parsley

2 cups fresh parsley leaves
vegetable oil for deep-frying
4–6 tablespoons butter
2 cups canned hominy, drained
salt and pepper to taste

Wash and shake dry 2 cups of parsley clusters, stems removed. In a wok or deep skillet, heat 1–2 inches of cooking oil. Drop parsley clusters into the oil, a few at a time, and remove quickly with slotted spoon (a 20–30-second fry is enough). Drain on paper towels. Melt butter in a separate saucepan, add hominy, and heat through. Season to taste, add parsley, and serve.
Serves 4.

MARMALADE,
BRITISH AND YANK

"March is the proper month for making this preserve," the Briton Eliza Acton wrote in 1861 in her *Modern Cookery*, "the Seville oranges being then in perfection." For the British the bitter Seville, once spelled and still pronounced "civil," is the only proper orange for making this preserve, in a land where marmalade proprieties rank high. For at least two centuries, every proper Britisher has begun his British day by savoring God, king, and country in this last preserve of empire—the pot of marmalade.

Seville oranges are as bitter as their Chinese progenitors of 2,300 years ago, "the bitter oranges of Chang-p'u," which Arab traders brought to Spain and Eleanor of Castile to England. During the Middle Ages these sun-kissed globes were status symbols exclusive to royal tables and orangeries. Queen Elizabeth I, with her addiction to candied orange peel and other sweetmeats, made sugared fruits the fashion for commoners aspiring to higher things.

Oranges, actually, were latecomers to the wide world of marmalade. That curious word was imported from Portugal, where *marmelo* meant quince, always a favorite fruit for jellying and preserving because it is high in pectin. English marmalades, which were really chunky jams, were made originally with cherries, pears, white and purple plums, white and red quinces, pippins or apples, raspberries—and oranges, if you could *gitt* them.

"Take the best sivill oringes you can gitt," Rebecca Price advised in *The Compleat Cook* in mid-seventeenth-century England, thus creating precepts for marmalade making followed across the seas a century later by Martha Washington. For her "Marmelet of Orringes" in *A Booke of Sweetmeats* (1749), Martha probably used oranges from Florida, where Ponce de León had planted Seville seeds as early as 1513. Three centuries later they were growing wild, as Maria Parloa explains in a recipe for "Sour Orange Preserve" in her 1872 *Appledore Cookbook*. "The orange used is not the common market orange," Maria says, "but the wild, sour orange found in Florida."

In Britain marmalade eventually became synonymous with Seville oranges through the proliferation of the industrialized preserve made by James Keiller in Dundee and Frank Cooper in Oxford. In America, marmalades were more eclectic. In *The Settlement Cook Book* of 1930, Lizzie Kander lists under *Marmalade* such mixtures as orange and peach, carrot and lemon, grapefruit and pineapple, grape and raisin. Today we even make marmalade of vegetable-fruits like green and red tomatoes. With any marmalade or jelly, boil the fruit in a relatively wide and shallow pan to hasten evaporation and use enamel or stainless steel to avoid discoloration. To increase natural pectin, add a quince or apple, cut in half, and discard it after the boiling.

Anglophiles in this country who whimper in March for the rites of marmalade making can get canned Seville oranges under the brand Mamade. Sometimes fresh Sevilles appear in specialty markets. But Yanks like me prefer to use the sweet navel orange of Brazil, which was first grown in my own hometown of Riverside, California, beside the palms and cacti. Navels, or Valencias, do not require the lengthy soakings advised by Martha Washington for Sevilles, "till ye bitterness by gon." Since citrus fruits vary in bitterness, I like to experiment with combinations of bitter and sweet, mixing pink grapefruit with orange and lime. I also like to fool with sweet and hot, as in another Southwest favorite, hot pepper jelly, which I've turned into a deeply red marmalade of sweet red bell peppers and whatever hot pepper is at hand.

I've always used marmalade as a sauce or binder with fresh or cooked fruits for dessert, such as quince and applesauce, apple slices fried in butter and laid into tarts, pears sliced and sautéed, or apricots stewed in honey and nuts. Here I've put a little marmalade into a light orange-and-carrot cake to substitute for the sugar overload that rots the teeth of the bran-and-yoghurt set.

Although the marmalade that sustained a proper British bear like Paddington on his trek to London from Peru had to be made from bitter oranges, Yanks need not be so civil. It was a Scottish Presbyterian missionary, after all, who in 1870 sent a dozen Navel saplings from Bahia to the States as a sweet alternative to the bitter fruits of empire.

True Brit Marmalade

3 pounds Seville oranges, fresh or canned
3 quarts water
5–6 pounds sugar (10 to 12 cups)

Wash the oranges and put them whole in a pot. Add the water, bring to a boil, and simmer, uncovered, about 1½ hours, or until the skin "can be pierced easily with the head of a pin." Remove the oranges and cut them in half, saving the water. Remove the seeds and tie them in cheesecloth. Cut the oranges into strips or into coarse chunks in a food processor. Return both oranges and seed bag to the water, add the sugar, and bring to a boil. Boil rapidly 15-25 minutes, until the syrup reaches the jelly stage (220° to 225°, or when a blob of liquid stiffens when dropped onto an ice cube). Discard the seeds and ladle the marmalade into scalded jars or pots.

Yields about 3 pints.

Red Pepper Marmalade

6 lemons
2 cups water
4 large sweet red bell peppers
4 small hot red or green peppers
½ cup cider or other fruit vinegar
4 cups sugar

Slice the lemons in quarters, remove seeds, and slice vertically. Cover with the water, bring to a boil, and simmer, covered, 20-30 minutes. Let sit overnight. Cut the large peppers in quarters lengthwise, remove seeds and stems, and cut flesh into strips or squares. Cut small hot peppers in half lengthwise, remove seeds and inner membranes, and mince the flesh. Add the peppers to the lemons, then add the vinegar and sugar, and boil rapidly 40-50 minutes, until jelly stage, stirring constantly as liquid thickens.

Yields about 2 pints.

Citrus Marmalade

1 large pink grapefruit
2 navel oranges
2 limes or lemons
2 cups water
5 cups sugar
1/4 cup Cointreau or Essencia* (optional)

Quarter the grapefruit and remove the rind. Discard the seeds and remove the pulp from the membranes. Cut the oranges in quarters, remove the rind, and add the orange pulp to the grapefruit. Scrape some of the white pith from inside the orange rinds and discard, then cut the rinds into strips. Cut the grapefruit rind into similar strips. Quarter the limes or lemons and slice each vertically into thin strips, rind and all. Remove the seeds. Put all pulp and rinds into a large pot with the water, bring to a boil, and simmer 20–30 minutes. Let stand 12 hours or overnight to soften the rind. Add the sugar and boil rapidly, 45–60 minutes, until the liquid reaches the jelly stage (220° to 225°). As the water evaporates, stir frequently to avoid scorching. Add Cointreau if desired and ladle the mixture into scalded jars.

Yields about 3 pints.

*Essencia is a relatively new Yankee dessert wine made from orange muscat grapes in California.

Marmalade Carrot Cake

3/4 cup (1 1/2 sticks) butter
3/4 cup sugar
3 eggs
2 cups unbleached flour
1 1/2 teaspoons baking powder
1/4 teaspoon salt
1/2 cup orange or citrus marmalade
1/2 cup cooked carrots, chopped fine
1/2 cup almonds, chopped coarsely
Glaze: 1/3 cup fresh orange juice;
   1/3 cup sugar

Cream butter and sugar by hand or in a food processor. Add the eggs and beat well. Sift the flour with the baking powder and salt. Stir into the egg mixture. Add the marmalade, carrots, and nuts. Turn into a well-buttered Bundt pan and bake at 325° for about an hour. Reverse the cake onto a plate. Heat the orange juice and sugar just long enough to dissolve the sugar and pour the syrup over the cake.

Serves 12-16.

April

April

THE SMELL OF PARSLEY

Parsley Soup

Parsley Salad

Deep-Fried Parsley

Green Sauce for Cold Meat or Fish

Tabbouleh

EASTER EGGS: ROE UPON ROE

Easter Egg Surprise

Caviar Sorrel Cream

Seafood Salad with Red or Golden Mayonnaise

Shad Roe "Sandwich"

Roe on Roe

SAVORING SEEDS

To Toast Watermelon (or Other) Seeds

Sesame Seed Soup

Enchiladas in Pumpkin Seed Sauce

Papaya Salad with Papaya Seed Dressing

Sunflower Seed Cookies

THE SMELL OF PARSLEY

When Emily, transported to heaven in Thornton Wilder's play *Our Town*, is asked what she misses most on earth, she says, "The smell of parsley." It's hard to imagine life without parsley. Parsley apparently was growing wild in the Mediterranean basin about the time man was. Parsley is to the Western world what coriander (sometimes called Chinese parsley) is to the Eastern, an herb so common and pervasive that like other ordinary things—spring and youth and small towns like Grover's Corners—we miss them only when they're gone.

I always grew two kinds of parsley in my garden—the plain-leafed kind the grocers call "Italian" and the curly-leafed kind, which for Americans seems to be the only way a cooked salmon or turkey can appear in public without looking nude. I made no headway with a third kind grown for its roots rather than leaves, the turnip-rooted parsley that looks like a skinny parsnip and tastes like celery root. As a lazy gardener, I owed a lot to parsley because the plants lasted two years without replanting, and because all winter long I could step outside, brush the snow off, and snip a green and curly top.

Medieval herbalists found all kinds of parsley as useful in medicine as in food. The seventeenth-century Nicholas Culpepper prescribed a paste of parsley seed and root, mixed with fennel, caraway, burnet, and saxifrage, for "the jaundice, falling-sickness, the dropsy, and

stone in the kidneys." Parsley was also a major ingredient in the green garden pottages of the Middle Ages and the pureed green garden sauces of the Elizabethan Age, when they were called "Garden Sass."

What Englishman even today would eat a dish of jellied eels or a leg of mutton without a parsleyed sauce? What Frenchman would eat a snail without a pool of parsley and garlic butter or a mussel without a broth of parsley and wine? What Italian would eat a veal shank without that sprinkling of parsley, garlic, and grated lemon peel they call *gremolata?* And what Moroccan would eat a salad of cracked wheat, or bulgur, unlaced with parsley and mint?

Because parsley is so often minced, the herb has developed its own line of kitchen hardware and impassioned ritual. For years I refused to use the efficient hand-cranked Mouli parsley grater because I liked the ritual of scrunching sprigs of curly-leafed parsley together and chopping them with a knife, either the old-fashioned double-handed chopper or a Chinese cleaver, and of cutting flat-leafed parsley with a pair of scissors. I know a Hollywood dowager, once a silent film star accused of murdering her lover, who fired her housekeeper for not mincing parsley fine enough. And I have a friend so obsessed with parsley that he keeps a mini spin-dryer exclusively for drying parsley leaves and a special rolling chopper for cutting them.

Despite our constant use of parsley as a garnish, we neglect it as a vegetable. On a hot spring day it makes a fine cold soup, a salad, or a sauce for thin slices of smoked tongue, ham, or beef, not to mention poached chicken and fish. Deep-fried it makes delicious finger food to serve with shellfish. And for a one-dish vegetarian meal, there's tabbouleh, which returns chopped parsley to its origins in the Middle East.

When we are tempted to take parsley too much for granted as our commonest garden herb, we might remember the moral pointed out in Beatrix Potter's rhyming tale:

> *Cecily Parsley lived in a pen,*
> *And brewed fine ale for gentlemen;*
> *Gentlemen came every day,*
> *'Til Cecily Parsley ran away.*

Parsley Soup

2 cups packed parsley leaves
6 cups chicken or fish stock
¼ cup uncooked rice
3 eggs
juice of 1 lemon
½–1 cup yoghurt

Wash parsley, remove the stems, and spin-dry the leaves. Mince leaves by hand or in a food processor. Meanwhile bring stock to a boil, add rice, and simmer, covered, about 15 minutes, or until rice is tender. Beat eggs with the lemon juice, stir in some of the hot broth, then add egg mixture to the pan and whisk rapidly over very low heat for a minute or two (higher heat will curdle the eggs). Off heat add parsley and yoghurt to taste. Refrigerate until wanted. (This soup is good hot, though, as well as cold.)
Serves 4-6.

Parsley Salad

5 cups curly- and flat-leafed parsley, mixed
1 cup bread cubes, cut in ¼-inch squares
3 garlic cloves, minced
½ cup good olive oil
1 tablespoon wine vinegar
pepper to taste
¼ pound feta cheese

Remove stems from parsley and put leaves in a covered steamer about 45 seconds to barely soften them. Refrigerate immediately to crisp. Make croutons from the bread cubes by sautéing them with the garlic in 2–3 tablespoons of the olive oil until brown. Mix remaining oil with vinegar and pepper, mix parsley with crumbled feta cheese, and sprinkle croutons on top.
Serves 4.

Deep-Fried Parsley

4 cups parsley leaves
vegetable oil for frying
salt to taste

Make sure parsley leaves are thoroughly dry. Drop a handful at a time into oil heated to 370°–375° in a wok or deep skillet and remove quickly, after less than a minute, with a slotted spoon. Drain leaves on paper towels. They should be crisp and green. Sprinkle lightly with salt.

Serve as a garnish or a finger-food snack.

Yields about 2 cups.

Green Sauce for Cold Meat or Fish

1 cup closely packed parsley leaves
1/2 cup watercress leaves
1/2 cup fresh herbs, such as chervil, tarragon,
    thyme, marjoram, chives
3 anchovy fillets
1 tablespoon capers
4 egg yolks, 1 raw and 3 hard-cooked
3/4–1 cup olive oil
3 tablespoons vinegar or lemon juice
pepper to taste

Rinse and spin-dry the parsley, watercress, and herbs; put them in a processor or blender with the anchovies, capers, and egg yolks, and chop coarsely. Add olive oil gradually, thin with vinegar or lemon juice, and season with pepper. To make sauce thicker add more parsley or watercress; to make thinner add more oil.

Yields about 2 cups sauce.

Tabbouleh

1½ cups bulgur wheat
1½ cups each flat- and curly-leafed parsley
½ cup fresh mint
¼ cup fresh coriander leaves
4 scallions, with green tops
12 cherry tomatoes, halved
½ cup olive oil
½ cup lemon juice
1 small hot pepper, minced
salt and pepper to taste
1 sweet red bell pepper
12 black Mediterranean-cured olives

Cover bulgur with boiling water and let stand 1 hour. Drain and spread on paper towels to dry. Chop parsley, mint, coriander, and scallions in a processor or by hand. Mix with the bulgur and tomatoes in a bowl. Mix the oil, lemon juice, hot pepper, and seasonings and pour over the bulgur. Lightly toss with fork or fingers. Cover with plastic wrap and refrigerate overnight, if possible. Cut the sweet pepper in thin strips and decorate top of salad with the pepper and olives.

Serves 4.

EASTER EGGS:
ROE UPON ROE

If you want bright-colored eggs for Easter, you don't have to dye chicken eggs or buy foil-wrapped eggs laid by chocolate bunnies. Nature produces the brightest eggs of all and with such wild abandon that we celebrate their source—the fish—as our most ancient symbol of fertility. For a real Easter-egg hunt, don't look under the bush but dive into the sea.

American seas once teemed with fish and eggs. "In the olden days all our people had to do to get food was to gather what the Great Nature provided," said an elderly member of the Gitksan tribe in British Columbia, where many Indians still live by their ancestral ways. Great Nature provided, in the olden days, sturgeon, salmon, whitefish, cod, flounder, shad, herring, scallops, crabs, and crayfish, all stuffed to the gills at spawning season with eggs of many colors. The cod furnished apple-pink roe, the sturgeon glistening black roe, the whitefish golden roe, and the salmon Chinese red.

Centuries before sturgeon roe became "caviare to the general," the American Indians were gathering and curing all kinds of fish eggs for their intense flavor and condensed nutrition. Even today, many Northwestern tribes harvest herring spawn by collecting the spawn on fir boughs or kelp. And many continue to cure fish eggs by the ancient method of fermenting them, just as the Chinese ferment duck eggs for their "hundred-year preserved eggs." The Gitksans smoke skeins of roe over alder wood, then wrap the skeins in birch bark, lay them in a box of cedar, and bury them in the earth until the eggs ripen like cheese.

Pioneers and settlers, however, were less respectful of this sea bounty. In the nineteenth century, sturgeon roe was so common in American rivers and seas that we shipped 100,000 pounds of caviar a year to Europe and saloon keepers in America gave it away free. Salmon roe was so common that salmon processors slapped it into cans and, by overpasteurizing and overbrining it, rendered it nearly inedible. Only recently has fresh salmon roe become available, though it is costly, in city fish markets; its delicate taste and texture are a revelation. Until recently whitefish roe was wretchedly overbrined and, worst of. all, dyed black to imitate caviar. Fortunately, a pair of Swedes who emigrated to San Francisco a decade ago now market fresh whitefish roe as "golden caviar."

American fishermen still wastefully dump the roe and milt (or sperm) of cod, flounder, and carp, just as they discard the delicious crescent orange roe of the sea scallop and save only the muscle. Although Americans are great eaters of shellfish, we often toss out with the shell the intense coral-colored roe of shrimp, crab, and lobster and only very recently have we begun to discover, with a little help from Japanese sushi bars, the hidden treasured eggs of the sea urchin.

With any roe, a little goes a long way because the taste is as intense as the color. Roe of any kind will enrich a sauce, a soup, an omelet, a mousse, a seafood salad, a pasta. Skeins of shad or cod roe make a rich entrée when sautéed gently in butter and discreetly herbed. Or they can enliven a baked potato, which serves as a convenient container; or fish fillets, which can serve as a sandwich. In cooking roe, there are only two don'ts: *don't* overcook fresh fish roe or it will become dry, grainy, and tasteless; and *don't* cook sturgeon or salmon roe at all or it will become strong and bitter.

In my recipes here I've suggested only a few of the many ways in which we can enrich our palates with different kinds of roe. And for fun I've included a surprise for Easter breakfast that gives the adults something to do while the kids are hunting all those chocolate eggs that the Easter Bunny, heedless of teeth, appetites, clothes, and complexions, has hidden for them.

Easter Egg Surprise

4 white hen's eggs
4 tablespoons black, red, or golden "caviar"
pepper to taste
4 egg cups

Hard-cook the eggs by covering them with cold water and bringing them slowly to a simmer. Remove from heat, cover, and let sit 20 minutes. Drain and cover with cold water until the shells are cool. With a sharp knife slice off the pointed end of each egg far enough up to remove the contents and yet retain most of the shell. Finely chop together white and yolk and season with pepper. Pack each shell with a tablespoon of "caviar," then the chopped egg. Reverse the shells into egg cups. Set each place with a sharp knife to crack the shell and a small spoon to remove contents.

Serves 4.

Caviar Sorrel Cream

½ cup fish stock or clam juice
½ cup dry white wine
1 cup heavy cream
¼ cup chopped green onions
black pepper to taste
⅓ cup pureed sorrel
2 tablespoons red or golden "caviar"

Mix stock, wine, cream, onions, and pepper and reduce liquid by half over high heat. Add sorrel and puree mixture in a blender until smooth. Stir in the caviar and refrigerate until cold and thick. Taste and add more caviar if wanted. Serve with homemade melba toast. (This also makes a fine fish sauce.)

Yields about 1½ cups.

Seafood Salad with Red or Golden Mayonnaise

½ pound shrimp in shells
¼ cup fish stock
¼ cup dry white wine
salt and pepper to taste
2–3 sprigs fresh coriander
1 pound sea scallops
1 ripe avocado
endive leaves

Simmer shrimp for 5 minutes in stock, wine, and seasonings. Remove and cool until you can peel the shells.

In the shrimp liquid, simmer the scallops about 4 minutes, or until barely done. Remove and cool. Peel the avocado and cut into cubes. Mix with the seafood and arrange in the center of a platter. Place endive leaves around the center like a sunburst. Serve with mayonnaise in a separate bowl.

Serves 4–8.

FOR THE MAYONNAISE:
1 whole egg
1 tablespoon Dijon mustard
¾ cup olive oil
1 tablespoon lemon juice
2 tablespoons red or golden "caviar"
sour cream or yoghurt (optional)

Blend egg with mustard in a food processor or blender. Slowly add oil until mixture thickens. Thin with lemon juice and fold in the "caviar." For a lighter mayonnaise, add a little sour cream or yoghurt.

Yields about 1 cup.

Shad Roe "Sandwich"

1 pair shad roe
4 tablespoons butter
2 or 3 sprigs fresh tarragon (or ½ teaspoon dried)
1 tablespoon lemon juice
salt and pepper
2 shad fillets
¼ cup chopped green onions
1 cup dry white wine

Poach roe gently, covered, in butter, tarragon, and lemon juice for about 5 minutes. Salt and pepper the fleshy side of each shad fillet. Enclose the roe within the "flaps" of one fillet and place other fillet on top. Place "sandwich" on large piece of buttered foil, sprinkle fish with onions, add wine to the foil container, and seal top. Bake at 400° for about 20 minutes. Remove fish to serving platter and reduce sauce, adding more butter, tarragon, and lemon juice if wanted.

Serves 6.

Roe on Roe

2 pair roe (shad, cod, flounder)
¼ cup chopped green onions
½ cup white wine
½ cup fish stock or clam juice
pepper to taste
½ pound (2 sticks) butter
½ cup sour cream or crème fraîche
4 baked potatoes
¼ cup black or red "caviar"
¼ cup chives

Poach roe gently, in a covered pan, with onions, wine, stock, and pepper for about 5 minutes. Remove roe and reduce liquid by half. Over low heat gradually beat in the butter, cut in pieces, until sauce thickens. Remove from heat and beat in the cream. Split the hot baked potatoes and place one roe in each. Pour sauce on top and sprinkle with caviar and chives.

Serves 4.

SAVORING SEEDS

It's odd to think that peas in a pod, corn on a cob, or coconuts on a palm are all seeds. Considering how much our very lives depend upon seeds, it's also odd that we should say of someone shabby that he is "seedy," or of a bad situation, "It's the pits." Evidently we have mixed feelings about seeds because seeds, from a cook's or eater's point of view, are a mixed blessing. There are seeds we savor, like peas, corn, and coconuts. There are seeds we tolerate for the sake of the pod, like those of tomatoes, cucumbers, and raspberries. There are seeds we throw away, like those of apple, grape, olive, and cherry. There are seeds we actively spit out, like watermelon, and there are seeds we curse, like mango.

Many seeds we cultivate for their power to flavor food, like nutmeg in its cage of mace; like anise distilled into Pernod, ouzo, and anisette; like caraway and mustard with their separate and distinctive bite. Other seeds we treat as foods in themselves, for the seeds that we most commonly think of as seeds, like sesame, sunflower, and pumpkin, are as rich in protein as they are in oil. Take the sesame seed, which from the time of ancient Greece has supplied much of the world with flavoring for breads and sweets, with oils for cooking, and with a dense paste the Middle East calls tahini, which is as rich and nourishing as peanut butter.

If Americans have learned the uses of sesame from Africa and the Middle East, our own continent and our own native inhabitants can teach us much about other kinds of seeds. For the American Indian, seeds were as essential a food as fish and game. Fortunately, sunflowers grew like weeds so Indians everywhere could harvest them by shaking the seeds from the giant heads, then parching and grinding them into meal. Sometimes they turned the meal into a mush, like corn, or brewed roasted seeds to make a drink like coffee. In his *Zuni Breadstuff*, Frank Hamilton Cushing describes how Zunis in the 1880s fashioned sunflower seeds "into little patti-cakes which, laid on leaves, or hardened by roasting deep buried in the ashes, were eaten with other food in the place of meat."

Since pumpkin and squash were almost as ubiquitous as sunflowers, Indians everywhere saved their seeds to use as a thickener, as we would use flour, or as an oily paste, as we would use butter. Where papayas grew, in the tropical Caribbean, the Carib Indians savored the black seeds nested within because they were as peppery in taste as the Asian peppercorn. Wherever watermelons grew, Indians salvaged their seeds to roast and nibble like popcorn.

In the recipes here, I've suggested a seedy, but by no means shabby, meal by using seeds in every course from soup to nutlike cookies, beginning with a watermelon seed snack. The soup is a traditional Southern one from Sarah Rutledge's *The Carolina Housewife* (1847), where she calls it "Bennie Soup." Bennie was the name slaves gave to the sesame seeds they brought with them from Africa. The main dish bakes enchiladas, stuffed with cheese that substitutes for Mexican *queso fresco*, in a pumpkin seed sauce based on a traditional *mole verde* from the Mayan Indians of Mexico. The salad dresses papaya and avocado with lime and papaya seeds. And for dessert, sweetened sunflower seed nuggets may remind us of the Zunis, for whom seeds were not the pits but as precious as pearls.

To Toast Watermelon (or Other) Seeds

Wash the seeds if necessary, blot them dry in paper towels, and toast them 3-5 minutes in an ungreased skillet, or about 10 minutes in a 300° oven. (Cover pumpkin seeds, for they are apt to pop.) For snack use, salt the seeds while still hot.

Sesame Seed Soup

1 cup toasted sesame seeds
4 cups fish stock or clam juice
1 pint oysters
1 small red chili pepper, minced
salt and black pepper to taste

Grind the seeds with 2 cups of the fish stock in a blender and add to remaining fish stock. Drain the oysters and add their liquor to the stock. Add red pepper and seasonings and bring to a simmer. Add oysters and simmer 2-3 minutes, or until oysters just begin to curl.
Serves 4.

Enchiladas in Pumpkin Seed Sauce

½ cup finely chopped onions
2 tablespoons corn oil
1 cup each ricotta and feta cheese
½ cup grated Monterey Jack cheese
½ cup sour cream
8 corn tortillas
vegetable oil for frying

FOR THE SAUCE:
1 cup raw pumpkin seeds
2 jalapeño or serrano peppers
2 cloves garlic, mashed
½ cup finely chopped onions
⅛ teaspoon cumin seeds
2 tablespoons vegetable oil
3 cups chicken broth
2-3 sprigs fresh coriander
salt and pepper to taste

Sauté the onions gently in the oil for about 2 minutes. Mix with the ricotta cheese, half the feta (reserve the rest for garnish), the Monterey Jack, and the sour cream. Soften each tortilla in an inch of vegetable oil heated in a skillet until hot but not smoking. Drain the tortillas, place some of the cheese mixture on each, and roll them up tightly. Place them seam side down in a greased baking dish large enough to hold them in a single layer.

Toast raw seeds in a heavy skillet 2–4 minutes, stirring them so they don't burn and covering them partially with a lid, since the seeds like to jump. Remove the seeds and reserve. Mince the peppers, mix them with the garlic, onions, and cumin, and sauté about 5 minutes in the oil. Turn this mixture into a blender, add the seeds, 2 cups chicken broth, plus coriander and salt and pepper, and puree the entire mixture. Thin with more broth as desired.

Bake the tortillas, uncovered, at 350° for 10 minutes to crisp them. Pour the sauce over them, sprinkle tops with the remaining feta cheese, cover the baking dish with foil or a lid, and bake 10–12 minutes, or until sauce is bubbling.

Serves 4.

Papaya Salad with Papaya Seed Dressing

1 ripe papaya
1 ripe avocado
1–2 navel oranges
1 red onion, sliced thin

Slice papaya in half and remove seeds. Pare off skin and slice fruit lengthwise into thin ¼-inch slices. Cut avocado in half, then quarters, discard pit, and remove skin. Cut in lengthwise slices. Peel and segment oranges. Alternate papaya and avocado slices with the segmented orange in the middle, surrounded with onion slices. Pour dressing over the whole.

Serves 4.

Papaya Seed Dressing

1 slice of papaya
2 teaspoons papaya seeds
⅓–½ cup olive oil
2 tablespoons lime or lemon juice
salt to taste

Put all ingredients in a blender and puree until smooth. The seeds will form black flecks like pepper.

Yields about ⅔ cup dressing.

Sunflower Seed Cookies

1 cup sunflower seeds
¾ cup (1½ sticks) butter
1½ cups dark brown sugar
1¼ cups flour
¼ teaspoon baking powder
¼ teaspoon salt
1 egg

Chop seeds roughly in a processor or blender. Mix well with the remaining ingredients (a processor works fine). Shape into ½-inch balls and place on a buttered baking sheet. Bake at 300° about 15 minutes, or until edges are browned.

Yields about 50 cookies.

May

SEXY ARTICHOKES AND ASPARAGUS

Artichoke Cups

Herbed Vinaigrette

Crisp Asparagus

Orange Hollandaise

Asparagus Italian Style

Eggs Artichoked or Asparagused

SPRINGING FOR LAMB

Lamb with a Spoon

Greek Butterflied Lamb

Roast Loin of Lamb

Braised Lamb Chops with Garlic and Olives

AVOCADO APHRODISIA

Avocado Béarnaise Sauce

Avocado-Yoghurt Dressing or Dip

Margarita Avocados

Avocado-Chili Soup

Green Tomato Guacamole

California Omelet

Avocado-Grapefruit Cream

SEXY ARTICHOKES
AND ASPARAGUS

"A" is for Artichokes and Asparagus, which stand first in our vegetable alphabet, first in our spring gardens, and first among the aristocrats of the vegetable kingdom. The Florentine Medici doted on artichokes, as did Roman Caesars on asparagus. They thought them potent—that armored orb, that naked spear—and downright sexy.

Sexy they are, not just in shape but in the fingered way we eat them. The one we strip leaf by leaf to reach its guarded bottom. The other we nibble, at length, from tip to butt. They turn our vegetable rape, perforce, into seduction. But of course you can resist. You can treat them like any old thistle and stalk designed to give you grief instead of pleasure. You can grouch at an artichoke's prickly leaf and choke at the cook who served you up this thistle. Or you can scorn an asparagus stalk as if your palate were too delicate for anything but its tender tip.

A cook faced with such barbarism can either fight or surrender. A wise cook compromises. He forestalls the artichoke grouch by removing the choke ahead of time to turn the globe into its own sauce boat. He forestalls the asparagus hack by peeling the stalks to make them as tender as the tips. These are small attentions that pay large dividends.

To turn an artichoke into a cup, cut off the top third of the globe (and, for fancy, clip off the top of each remaining leaf with scissors) before boiling it. Once the

globe is cooked and drained, spread the leaves apart, remove the center core, and scrape out the fuzzy choke with a pointed teaspoon.

To peel asparagus, first snap the stalk to remove the tough end, then strip the outer skin with a vegetable peeler to an inch below the beginning of the tips. Don't worry about waste because you can throw the peelings into a plastic bag and freeze them for a later soup.

As for boiling or steaming, results are the same in taste, texture, and nutrients. Water does not wash away the potassium of artichokes or the vitamin A of asparagus. Overcooking, however, washes away texture as well as taste. Fortunately, we no longer heed the directives of nineteenth-century ladies like Miss Eliza Leslie, who wanted her artichokes boiled two hours and her asparagus one. An artichoke will take anywhere from 25 to 45 minutes before its bottom is easily pierced with a knife. A peeled asparagus will take only 3 to 8 minutes before its tip wobbles slightly and begins to droop if you fork up a stalk and shake it.

The one advantage of steaming artichokes, rather than boiling them, is that the globes bobble on the top of a boiling pot. But you can poke them under from time to time or set a large sieve or colander into the top of your pot. Special asparagus steamers, which were all the rage in the 1930s, are wholly unnecessary. Both James Beard and Julia Child cook their asparagus in a flat pan, like a skillet, and boil them uncovered. You don't need to tie the spears into bundles and, with peeled stalks, you don't need to worry about stalks and tips cooking unevenly.

Good draining to avoid watery plates is essential for both vegetables. Turn artichokes upside down to drain. With asparagus, I drain them first in a colander and then spread them on paper or linen towels. Some of our grandmothers used a porcelain asparagus plate pierced with holes, but another old-fashioned device which is both elegant and practical is to serve unsauced asparagus on a white linen napkin.

I like to serve both vegetables at room temperature in a dressing so simple it bares the sexiness of each. The same sauces flatter both, whether a pungent oil-and-vinegar dressing or an oil-and-egg emollient like mayonnaise or hollandaise. To vary a classic vinaigrette, here I've added anchovy, capers, and a garden herb such as basil or chives. To vary a hollandaise, I've used orange juice and rind, in a sauce the French call *maltaise*. Sometimes I fold in a little sour cream or whipped heavy cream for a *mousseline*. The Italians favor oil and Parmesan cheese, the English melted butter with a sprinkling of finely chopped hard-cooked eggs. When feeling lavish, I use chopped walnuts and walnut oil.

If you can buy them or grow them, baby artichokes are as wonderful to eat raw as those slender asparagus stalks called "spaghetti grass." Serve both with drinks, with a sauce for a dip. Either vegetable, when cooked, is a course of its own and can be a meal in itself. But if your garden or grocer has gone mad this May with artichokes and asparagus, do as the Florentine and Roman emperors did. Take only the delicate bottoms or tips and nest them in eggs. It's a good way to use leftovers and to unman forever the grouch and hack at your table.

Artichoke Cups

Use 1 artichoke per person. Cut off stem and small leaves at base. Cut off top one-third of the way down. Rub lemon on cut surfaces to keep them from darkening. Boil, uncov-

ered, in a large pot of salted water 25–45 minutes, or until a knife will easily pierce the base. Drain upside down. Remove the center cone of leaves and dig out the choke with a sharp teaspoon. Set artichoke upright on a plate and fill with vinaigrette or hollandaise.

Herbed Vinaigrette

⅔ cup good olive oil
1 anchovy fillet, mashed
2–3 tablespoons lemon juice or vinegar
⅓ cup large capers, drained
⅓ cup chopped fresh basil, chives, or parsley
pepper to taste

Gradually stir oil into the mashed anchovy. Add lemon juice or vinegar to taste, along with capers, herbs, and pepper.
Yields about 1 cup.

Crisp Asparagus

Estimate 24 large spears or 2 pounds for 4 servings. Snap off butt ends where the stalk breaks. Peel each stalk from the bottom to about one inch from the tip. Cut off the ends evenly. Lay the spears in a deep skillet and cover with salted, boiling water. Boil, uncovered, 5–8 minutes, or until the tips droop slightly when shaken. Drain well.

Orange Hollandaise

3 egg yolks
1 tablespoon lemon juice
2 tablespoons orange juice
½ teaspoon salt, or to taste
¼ pound (1 stick) butter
2 tablespoons orange rind, finely chopped

Put yolks with juices and salt in a blender or processor, or beat by hand. Blend or process for about 10 seconds. Heat butter until it starts to bubble and, while it is still bubbling, pour it slowly through the opening in the lid of blender or processor until sauce thickens, or beat in butter by hand. Mix in the orange rind and taste for seasoning.

Yields about 1 cup.

Asparagus Italian Style

2 pounds cooked asparagus
½ cup warmed olive oil
a few drops lemon juice or balsamic vinegar
½ cup grated Parmesan cheese
4-8 slices prosciutto

For 4 servings, put 6 spears on each plate. Cover tips with oil mixed with juice and sprinkle with cheese. Cover stalks with 1-2 slices prosciutto.

Eggs Artichoked or Asparagused

8–10 eggs
4 tablespoons butter
4 cooked artichoke bottoms or 16 cooked
    asparagus tips
salt and pepper to taste
¼ cup chopped fresh tarragon, chives, or parsley
4 slices toast, cut in triangles

For 4 servings, scramble eggs gently in butter and divide among 4 plates. Nest artichoke bottoms, cubed, or asparagus tips, on top of the eggs, sprinkle with seasonings and herbs, and garnish with buttered toast points. (Make artichoke bottoms by cooking the artichoke whole, then removing leaves and choke. Don't worry about the waste of leaves. Their total yield is less than a teaspoon of edible "flesh.")

SPRINGING FOR LAMB

How can we account for the American disinclination to eat lamb? Where the average American carnivore devours 77.2 pounds of beef and 65 pounds of pork each year, he eats a trifling 1.4 pounds of lamb. And he eats most of that at Easter, when he succumbs or at least nods to history and to the paschal roast favored by gods as ancient and as disparate as Yahweh, Apollo, Christ, Allah, and Shiva.

Americans the rest of the year are "sulky towards lamb," according to the food historian Waverley Root, because we have overcommercialized and standardized lamb until it lacks all variety. Only those lucky ones who raise their own sheep can get the delicate sucklings beloved of the French, who nibble baby lamb chops no bigger than your thumb. Only sheep farmers can get the mutton beloved of the Victorian English and their American followers such as Marion Harland. In her 1878 *Dinner Year-Book*, Mrs. Harland climaxes her grand Company Dinner for April (after the Oysters, Ox-Head Soup, Baked Shad, Sweetbread Pâté, and Snipe on Toast) with a Boiled Leg of Mutton in Caper Sauce.

It's getting easier to wangle a rack of baby chops from my local butcher nowadays, but I've yet to see a saddle of mutton. Unfortunately, we are sold all year long a lamb labeled "spring," even though the lamb may be a year old and weigh upwards of 100 pounds. But if the label is spurious, the meat is certainly an improvement on the Depression lamb of my youth. Maybe that accounts for the American prejudice against lamb. What my family called "lamb" was an odoriferous gray lump boiled with string beans until both beans and meat were soft and stringy. Only from a rich friend did I learn that lamb also came in the form of chops, which you had to cut with a knife and were required to chew. Not until I reached England did I learn that lamb came in the form of crowns and saddles and barons. Not until I reached France did I discover that lamb might be flavored by the salt marshes of Brittany, by rosemary and garlic, and that it might be wrapped in buttery crusts. Only in Greece did I savor a whole spit-roasted Easter lamb, baptized with yoghurt and anointed with wine.

Perhaps the American neglect of lamb stems not from its standardized taste but from fear of carving a Sunday roast. One way to eliminate carving is to bake a leg of lamb for several hours until the meat is so tender you can scoop it out with a spoon. Another way is to have the butcher bone the leg and "butterfly" it so that the meat can be marinated and grilled like a steak. In the marinating, you can evoke France with Provençal herbs or Greece with yoghurt and lemon. A boneless loin roast is a costlier cut (a butcher bones a loin from the saddle), but is also a classically perfect one and a snap to carve. Finally, you can resort to a chop and can vary its flavor and texture by braising with roasted garlic and olives and interesting vegetables for a heady one-dish meal.

If the lamb we eat, like many of us who eat it, is not quite as youthful as spring, we can yet celebrate the greening of the year, each year, by rejoicing in lamb at all seasons.

Lamb with a Spoon

One 6–9-pound leg of lamb
½–1 cup sliced carrots
½–1 cup sliced onions
olive oil
Seasonings: salt and pepper, parsley, thyme,
    rosemary, bay leaf, or other mixed herbs
1½ cups stock or white wine

Trim leg of skin and fat and place in a roasting pan with the carrots and onions. Rub the top of the roast with a little olive oil and season to taste with salt, pepper, and herbs. Roast at 375° for about 30 minutes, or until meat is browned. Pour boiling stock or wine into the pan and cover meat loosely with foil. Reduce heat to 300° and bake 4–5 hours, until the meat is tender enough to cut with a serving spoon. For gravy, add more stock, if needed, to the pan juices and strain.

Serves 8–10.

Greek Butterflied Lamb

One 6–9-pound leg of lamb, boned and flattened
2–3 cups yoghurt
½ cup olive oil
juice of 2 lemons
3 cloves garlic, mashed (optional)
pepper and parsley or dill to taste

Remove all fat, skin, and gristle. Where meat is
thickest, cut 2 or 3 gashes so that meat will cook evenly.
Beat together yoghurt, oil, lemon juice, garlic, and seasonings and place the marinade in a large plastic bag with
the lamb. Massage the bag so that the lamb is covered
well on all sides. Let stand at room temperature for
several hours or refrigerate overnight. Grill over charcoal
or under a broiler, allowing 40-60 minutes. Meat should
be crusty on the outside and rare within.

Serves 8-10.

Roast Loin of Lamb

One 2-3-pound loin roast of lamb, boned and
    rolled (1¾ pounds after boning)
2 tablespoons olive oil
1 teaspoon soy sauce
pepper, dried rosemary, and thyme to taste
½ cup Dijon mustard

Roast should be well trimmed of fat and should be at
room temperature. Beat olive oil, soy sauce, and seasonings to taste into the mustard and coat top of meat with
the mixture. Roast at 450° for 10 minutes. Reduce heat to
425° and cook 10-20 minutes longer. The crust should be
very brown and the interior very pink, 120° on a meat
thermometer.

Serves 4.

Braised Lamb Chops with Garlic and Olives

1 whole head garlic
⅓ cup olive oil
2 sweet red bell peppers
2 large Belgian endives
8 small new potatoes
12 green olives
Seasonings: salt and pepper, thyme, rosemary,
   oregano, and bay leaf to taste
4 loin lamb chops, each 1½ inches thick

Separate the head of garlic into cloves, cover them with oil in a small baking dish, and bake them with their skins on for an hour at 300°. When cloves have cooled, skin them and return them to the oil. Seed and cut the red peppers in eighths and the endives in halves, and place them in a large baking dish with the potatoes, olives, garlic, and oil. Sprinkle with seasonings to your taste, cover dish tightly with foil, and bake at 325° about 45 minutes, or until potatoes are tender. Sear lamb chops quickly over high heat in a skillet (about 3 minutes to a side) and turn chops on their edges to brown the fat well. Put chops in the baking dish with the vegetables, season the chops, cover dish again with the foil, and bake at 325° about 15–20 minutes, or until chops are tender but still pink and juicy inside.

   Serves 4.

AVOCADO APHRODISIA

In spring, wherever a young man's fancy turns, mine turns to thoughts of food. Sexy food, to be sure, but food first, love second. While a gardener may think of green asparagus, a cook freed of geographic restraint may fantasize globes of green butter, neatly wrapped in green or black skins and hung in pairs on trees the Aztecs called *ahuacacuahatl*, or the "testicle tree." We call it avocado.

Mexican and Central American Indians discovered how to cultivate this sensual fruit 7,000 years ago, but it reached our shores only by the ships of Spanish and English explorers. Sixteenth-century Spaniards called the fruit *aguacate*, Englishmen called it "midshipman's butter," and anglicized Jamaicans "alligator pear." Like the banana, the avocado was too costly and too weird to be popular with Americans until this century. Avocados were not even planted here until Henry Perrine imported the West Indian variety to Florida in 1833 and Judge Ord the Mexican and Guatemalan varieties to California in 1871.

Even so, cooks were slow to catch on. Where Aztecs had mashed the pulp with tomatoes and chilies for *guacamole* (literally "avocado sauce") to serve with crisply grilled agave worms, the British tried to domesticate this strange fruit with Worcestershire sauce, and we Americans with ketchup and mayonnaise. Only after World War II did we begin to expand avocado uses beyond the standard alligator pear salad with pink dressing, or the rock-hard container of a seafood cocktail.

Californians, however, had a head start on the coming avocado boom. As a California child, I date my culinary coming of age from a spring day when I received from a handsome young man a crate of avocados, one for each day of the month. As the month progressed, my thoughts—my very person—turned fat, green, and pear-shaped, as I threw avocados into omelets, ice creams, chiffon pies, creamed chicken and crab, hamburgers, BLTs, and, yes, dear reader, even mashed potatoes. That crate liberated me forever from alligator pear salads.

Purists of course will insist that the only proper way to treat an avocado is to eat it plain, a free-standing meal on the half shell, with a lot of lime juice squeezed into the cavity and a freckling of black pepper on the flesh. But my avocado thoughts are never pure, especially not in spring. Here I've added tequila to the lime and rimed the fruit with salt to evoke a margarita. Helen Brown in her *West Coast Cook Book* (1952) poured rum into the avocado's hollow, but I could fancy reversing the process, whipping avocado into rum, to make an avocado daiquiri.

To a classic avocado soup I've added garlic and chili for heft. In a classic guacamole I've used Mexican *tomatillos* (Spanish groceries have them) or American green tomatoes. To a classic Brazilian dessert I've added honey and grapefruit pulp (or sometimes fresh pineapple) for texture and body. I could also fancy a California omelet with avocado and crab or a raw avocado stuffed with scallops seviche or a new-wave salad of avocado, papaya, and prosciutto.

I love avocados because they are sexy, but they are also good for you. Although they contain 25 percent fat, they also contain more protein than any other vegetable-fruit and they're packed with vitamin B and minerals. An anomalous fruit, they ripen only when removed from the tree, so you should expect to buy them unripe in the market and ripen them at home. To test for ripeness, squeeze the fruit gently in the palm of your hand or press the stem end to see if it's soft. To hasten ripening, put the fruit in a paper bag with a banana. Once the fruit is ripe, don't refrigerate it or it will darken. Once the fruit is cut, squeeze citrus juice over the cut surface and wrap it tightly in plastic wrap to delay darkening. You can heat it but don't cook avocado or it will turn bitter.

In spring an avocado is a green thought in a green shade. Treat it gently and it will prove to be, like music, food for love.

Avocado Béarnaise Sauce

1/4 cup vinegar
1/2 teaspoon dried chervil
1 teaspoon dried tarragon
1 tablespoon minced green onions or shallots
white pepper to taste
2 egg yolks
1 ripe avocado
1 tablespoon lemon juice
3/4 cup (1 1/2 sticks) butter

Boil vinegar with chervil, tarragon, onions, and pepper until reduced by half. Put reduced vinegar with herbs in a blender or processor. Add egg yolks, avocado, and lemon juice and blend. Heat butter until bubbling and pour it slowly through opening in the lid while the machine is on, until the mixture thickens like mayonnaise.

Yields 2 1/2–3 cups.

Avocado-Yoghurt Dressing or Dip

1/2 cup yoghurt or sour cream
1/4 ripe avocado
1 tablespoon minced onion
2 tablespoons lime or lemon juice
1 teaspoon salt
1/2 teaspoon ground cumin
1/4 teaspoon cayenne pepper

Put all ingredients in the order listed in a blender and puree until smooth. For a dip, increase yoghurt to 1 cup and increase hot pepper to taste.

Yields about 1 cup.

Margarita Avocados

1 ripe avocado
2 shot glasses of tequila
2 tablespoons fresh lime juice
1 teaspoon Triple Sec (optional)
salt to taste

Cut avocado in half and remove the pit. Mix the tequila, lime juice, and optional liqueur and pour into the cavity of each half. Sprinkle the flesh with salt.

Serves 2.

Avocado-Chili Soup

6 cups chicken or fish stock
1 cup heavy cream
1 clove garlic, mashed
1 tablespoon pure ground chili, or to taste
salt and pepper to taste
2 ripe avocados
2 tablespoons chopped fresh coriander

Bring the stock to a boil with the cream, garlic, and seasonings. Cut avocados in quarters and peel, then put the flesh in a blender. Add half the boiling stock and puree until smooth, then mix with remaining stock and pour into soup bowls. Garnish with coriander leaves. Equally good hot or cold.
Serves 6–8.

Green Tomato Guacamole

2 ripe avocados
4 *tomatillos* (or 2 green tomatoes)
1 tablespoon chopped onion
1 fresh serrano or jalapeño chili (or 3 canned
    chilis), minced
2 tablespoons lime or lemon juice
1 tablespoon chopped fresh coriander
salt and pepper to taste

Mash avocado pulp roughly with a fork to keep it chunky. Remove husks from the *tomatillos* and parboil

2 minutes; drain well and chop. (For green tomatoes, cut them in quarters, squeeze out the seeds, and chop.) Add tomatoes to the avocado, along with the onion, chili, lime juice, coriander, and seasonings. Sprinkle top with more coriander or a little pure ground chili.

Serves 4–8.

California Omelet
(after Helen Brown)

1 clove garlic, mashed
2 tablespoons olive oil
½ cup heavy cream
2 tomatoes, peeled, seeded, and chopped
12 ripe green olives, pitted and chopped
1 avocado, cubed
6 eggs
salt and pepper to taste
2 tablespoons butter

Heat garlic in the oil and cream until liquid simmers, then puree in a blender. Return mixture to the pan and add tomatoes, olives, and avocado. Keep mixture warm while making the omelet. Beat eggs with salt and pepper while heating the butter until bubbly in a large omelet pan. Pour in the eggs just before the butter browns and shake over high heat until a skin is formed on the bottom and the top begins to thicken. Add a third of the avocado mixture and fold the omelet over it. Pour remaining mixture onto a serving platter, roll the omelet from the pan onto the platter, and serve.

Serves 3–4.

Avocado-Grapefruit Cream

½ grapefruit
1 ripe avocado
2–3 tablespoons fresh lime juice
2–3 tablespoons honey

Remove grapefruit sections from their membranes and put pulp in a food processor or blender. Add the avocado flesh with the lime juice and honey, and puree until smooth. Taste for sweetness and sourness and add more lime or honey as necessary.
Serves 2–4.

June

June

SWEET PEAS

Peas with Rice (*Risi e Bisi*)

Peas with Mint

Peas with Basil (*Soupe au Pistou*)

Peas with Shrimp

CHICKENED IN

Cock-a-Leekie

Chinese Chicken and Noodles in Sesame Sauce

Lemon-Garlic Chicken with Artichokes and Olives

WILD AND WEEDY GREENS

Greens with Ham, Orange, and Mint

Chinese Stir-Fried Mustard Greens

Pickled Purslane Salad

Greens with Polenta

SWEET PEAS

Of all the vegetables he tended in his garden at Monticello, Thomas Jefferson most loved his sweet June peas. The notations in his *Garden Book* for the spring of 1774 have the urgency of military dispatches. "May 16. First dish of peas from earliest patch. May 26. A second patch of peas comes to table." On June 5, a third and fourth patch; on June 13, a fifth. By July 13, the battle was won and lost. "Last dish of peas."

In Jefferson's day, garden peas eaten young and fresh were as exotic a luxury as truffles are today. Until the middle of the seventeenth century, peas were grown solely for their dried seeds, to make the pease-porridges, pottages, puddings, and breads that were the staple foods of the Middle Ages. The craze for fresh peas started with the doges of Venice, who began to celebrate the feast day of St. Mark on April 25 with a rich broth of rice and fresh green peas, which they called *risi e bisi.*

When Italians introduced their spring peas, or *piselli novelli,* to the court of Louis XIV in France in 1660, they were a sensation. "It is a fashion, a fury," Madame de Sévigné wrote thirty years later of the court's obsession with *petits pois.* She wrote of the "impatience to eat them, the pleasure of having eaten them, the joy of eating them again." It was the French who established the classic method of cooking these tiny new peas by "sweating" them in butter, with greens like parsley and lettuce and a lump of sugar.

The English court took to fresh peas with the avidity of the French, but preferred to sweat their peas with mint. Both French and English gardeners went to work developing varieties of peas with an ever sweeter seed wrapped in an ever more tender pod. The result was the edible-podded sugar pea, which the French descriptively call *mange-tout* ("eat all") and the Chinese, snow pea.

Jefferson cultivated some thirty varieties of peas in his pea patch, among them the sugar pea, which, Amelia Simmons notes in her 1796 *American Cookery*, "needs no bush, the pods are tender and good to eat." Were Jefferson alive today, he might cultivate exclusively the Sugar Snap pea, a hybrid America introduced in 1979, which has the snap of a fresh green bean and the sweetness of a sugar pea. The Sugar Snap has, in turn, bred offspring called Sugar Daddy, Sugar Ann, and Sugar Rae. We still like our peas sweet.

Any gardener knows that the sugar in peas, like the sugar in sweet corn, turns quickly to starch. The shorter the trip from garden to table, the better the taste. "To have them in perfection," Virginia Randolph advises in *The Virginia Housewife* (1824), "they must be quite young, gathered early in the morning, kept in a cool place, and not shelled until they are to be dressed."

Only when they are young and extremely fine are they fit to be sweated in the French manner, which Louis Eustache Ude outlines in *The French Cook* (1828). Since M. Ude had been chef to both Louis XVI and the Duke of York, he could speak with authority on the royal craze for peas. The French fashion, Ude tells us, was to throw 3 quarts of peas into a bowl with ¼ pound of butter and lots of cold water in order to work the peas into the butter. The buttery mass then went into a pan with a layer of parsley and green onions and a powdering of sugar and flour.

In the recipes here, I've chosen the English method of sweating buttery peas with mint rather than parsley, but I've nodded to French tradition in a fresh-pea version of *Soupe au Pistou*. *Pistou* is Provençal for *pesto*, and the mingling of basil, garlic, and oil with green garden vegetables makes a fine vegetarian meal. Since most of us know edible-podded peas through Chinese dishes, I've also included a recipe that combines the glossy green of snow peas with the delicate pink of shrimp in a quick stir-fry that is good at any temperature.

In keeping with his love for all things French, Jefferson, as was the custom a century before his time, held an annual pea-patch competition with his neighbors at Monticello to bring the first dish of peas to the dinner table, where the winner invited his defeated rivals as guests. Year after year Jefferson was defeated by Mr. George Divers, but one spring Jefferson's patch was ready first and his family urged him to send off the ritual invitation. "No, say nothing about it," Jefferson answered, tucking into the first dish of peas. "It will be more agreeable to our friend to think that he never fails." Some Jeffersonians cite this as an example of Jefferson's generosity of spirit, but I say it was greed. Mr. Divers may have had the honor, but Jefferson had the peas.

Peas with Rice
(Risi e Bisi)

4 green onions, chopped
4 tablespoons butter
2 cups shelled peas (2 pounds unshelled)
4 cups hot chicken broth
1 cup short-grained rice (arborio)
2 tablespoons minced parsley
salt to taste
1/2 cup freshly grated Parmesan cheese

Chop both the white and green of the onions and sauté them gently in the butter in a deep saucepan with a lid. Add the peas and cook 1-2 minutes, stirring constantly. Add the hot broth, cover, and simmer 8-10 minutes. Add rice and parsley, stir once, bring to a boil, cover, and reduce heat to a simmer. Cook about 15 minutes. Taste for seasoning and add salt if needed. Stir in the cheese.
Serves 4.

Peas with Mint

1 bunch mint
4 cups shelled peas (4 pounds unshelled)
1 bunch green onions, chopped
1/4 pound (1 stick) butter
salt, pepper, and sugar to taste
1/2 cup heavy cream, whipped

Cover bottom of saucepan with 1/2-inch of water. Put in a layer of mint, saving a few leaves for garnish. Chop the remaining leaves and put aside. Add peas, onions, butter, and seasonings. Bring water quickly to a boil, cover tightly, and cook over moderate heat 5-10 minutes, or until peas are tender. Strain peas and save liquid. Discard the mint. Taste liquid for seasoning and reduce liquid if necessary. Add to peas and top them with a large dollop of heavy cream, sprinkled with chopped mint.

Serves 4-6.

Peas with Basil
(Soupe au Pistou)

1½ quarts chicken broth
1 cup shelled fresh lima beans
1 cup chopped leeks
1 cup string beans, cut in halves
1 cup diced young zucchini
2 cups Sugar Snap or snow peas
salt and pepper to taste

FOR THE PESTO:
4 cups basil leaves
½ cup parsley
2-3 cloves garlic, mashed
¾ cup olive oil
4 tablespoons butter, softened
½ cup grated Parmesan cheese

Bring broth to a boil, add lima beans and leeks, and simmer 8-10 minutes. Add string beans, then zucchini, and simmer 5 minutes. Add peas and cook 2-3 minutes for Sugar Snaps, or 1 minute only for snow peas. Add salt and pepper to taste. For the pesto, pack basil, parsley, garlic, oil, and butter in blender or food processor and process until leaves are chopped. Remove to a bowl and stir in the cheese. Stir sauce into hot soup and serve immediately.

Serves 6-8.

Peas with Shrimp

½ pound snow peas
1 pound shrimp
¼ cup peanut oil
1 clove garlic, minced
1 tablespoon fresh ginger root, minced
½ small fresh chili pepper, seeded and minced
½ teaspoon salt
4 green onions with tops, chopped
½ sweet red bell pepper, seeded and slivered
2 teaspoons sesame oil
1 teaspoon wine vinegar

Trim snow peas and shell shrimp. Heat oil in a wok or cast-iron skillet and add garlic, ginger, chili pepper, salt, and green onions. Stir 2 minutes. Add shrimp, keep fire hot, and stir shrimp constantly until they are pink (3-4 minutes). Add snow peas and slivers of red bell pepper and sauté 1 minute. Combine sesame oil and vinegar, pour over the shrimp and peas, and serve hot or at room temperature.

Serves 4.

CHICKENED IN

I have a friend who suffers from an incurable malady. He doesn't like chicken. He got chickened out, he says, during the Depression. I was luckier because I was poorer. In my house chicken was a ritual feast on Sunday, after church. The ritual began on Saturday when my grandfather chased our meal around the yard until he snagged it, wrung its neck, and plucked its feathers. I watched this rite with joy and terror—joy for the meal to come, terror lest the one chosen be my pet hen, Minnie, who tolerated a daily pull in my little red wagon.

In the days when we were still allowed to raise chickens in a city yard, chickens had a seasonal taste. In spring and summer, chickens tasted of new growth, for they had scratched up newly hatched beetles and worms and newly sprung grass to spice their diet of corn. What lent them flavor saved us money, and we little dreamed that the chickens we allowed to range free, for thrift, would one day be a luxury as rare as an egg fresh from the nest.

Even battery-fed chicken, however, has managed to survive the degradation of its factory enslavement and to maintain the status the bird has enjoyed since the first red jungle fowl was tamed in India 4,000 years ago. Because the chicken has adapted itself to the weathers, methods, and flavors of every country in the world, it is the most versatile, ubiquitous, and democratic of all our meats.

You can roast, poach, grill, steam, sauté, or fry it. You can dress it up or down. You can make a chicken-foot soup for the pineys of New Jersey or a truffled *poularde de Bresse* for the toffs of Paris. Four centuries apart, both Henri IV of France and Herbert Hoover of America named the chicken when they promised better times and the right of every man to a good dinner from the pot.

As a child my favorite dinner was chicken fried in a pot of Crisco and seasoned with pepper and salt. I didn't know that Mexico flavored its chickens with hot chilies, China with sesame and soy, India with turmeric and cardamom, Italy with sweet peppers and fresh tomatoes, Morocco with cinnamon and prunes, Turkey with walnuts, Spain with artichokes, and France with calvados or champagne. I did know, however, that the one rule of chicken was not to overcook it, since no flavor could redeem a dry and stringy hunk of flesh. I am certain that the chicken malaise suffered by my friend is the result of childhood abuse from overcooked chicken.

To demonstrate a chicken's infinite variety, I've chosen three recipes from around the world. From Scotland there's Cock-a-Leekie, a soup-stew dating back to the Middle Ages and combining the unusual flavors of leeks and prunes. Sir Walter Scott found this combination so royal that he had James VI announce, "Come, my lords and lieges, let us all to dinner, for the cocky-leeky is a-cooling."

From the Mediterranean I've chosen the pungent flavors of artichokes, garlic, lemons, and green olives to enhance a bird braised in a clay pot, a brown roasting bag, or any casserole with a tight lid. From China I've combined chicken, shredded and fried, with noodles cloaked in a mildly hot sesame sauce. A good source for other Chinese ways with chicken, such as chicken smoked in a wok, is Karen Lee's *Chinese Cooking Secrets* (1983).

Such flavors are far from the simple conclusion of my family's Sunday chicken dinner in Monday's chicken soup. On Monday my grandmother would add to the pot of simmering chicken feet and giblets whatever was left of skin and bone, along with vegetables and a marrow bone, if she had it. We were proud to fulfill Herbert Hoover's promise. And when at last my own Minnie, no longer a spring chicken but a matron in her prime, succumbed to that same pot, I seasoned her with a few salt tears and ate her, I confess, with relish.

Cock-a-Leekie

½ pound pitted prunes
One 3-pound chicken
8 cups beef stock or 2 pounds beef soup bones
2 bunches leeks
salt and pepper to taste

Soak prunes overnight or until soft. Fit chicken in a pot and cover with stock or soup bones and water. Bring to a simmer and skim foam from the top. Clean leeks well and add one bunch to the pot, cover partially, and simmer 20 minutes. Add remaining leeks, sliced in 3-inch lengths, and prunes, cut in strips. Season broth to taste and simmer 20–30 minutes, or until chicken is fork tender. Fill each soup bowl with broth and 2 or 3 slices of chicken, and garnish with prunes and leeks. Or serve broth for a first course and carve chicken for the main dish.
Serves 4–8.

Chinese Chicken and Noodles
in Sesame Sauce

1 pound chicken breasts, boned and skinned

MARINADE:
1 egg white
1 tablespoon sherry
1 tablespoon arrowroot or cornstarch
1 tablespoon each minced garlic and ginger root
1 small red chili pepper, minced
1/2 cup shredded green onions

SAUCE:
1/2 cup tahini (sesame seed paste)
2/3 cup black China tea
11/2 tablespoons soy sauce
1 tablespoon each sugar and red wine vinegar

2 cups vegetable or peanut oil for frying
1/2 pound egg noodles (preferably fresh)
1 tablespoon sesame oil

Freeze chicken breasts just long enough so that you can easily slice them lengthwise and shred the slices. Marinate the shredded chicken overnight in the combined ingredients of the marinade. Blend the ingredients for the sauce in blender or processor and reserve.

Heat 2 cups vegetable or peanut oil in a wok or cast-iron skillet until hot but not smoking (325°) and fry chicken rapidly, stirring, about 1 minute. Drain chicken in a colander and arrange in the middle of a serving platter.

Cook noodles until tender in boiling water. Drain and mix with the sesame oil. Surround the chicken with the noodles and pour sesame sauce over the whole. This is best at room temperature.

Serves 4-6.

Lemon-Garlic Chicken with Artichokes and Olives

One 3-4-pound roasting chicken
1 large onion, quartered
3-4 garlic cloves
2 lemons
2 tablespoons olive oil
salt and pepper to taste
2 large or 4 small artichokes
1 cup ripe green olives

Stuff cavity of chicken with onion, garlic, and 1 lemon, quartered. Rub outside of chicken with oil, season with salt and pepper, and place in a clay pot, oven bag, or small casserole with a lid. Surround chicken with quartered or halved artichokes, chokes removed, and with green olives. Slice remaining lemon and arrange over top of chicken. Cover pot or casserole and bake at 400° for 1 hour without removing lid. Test for tenderness and bake another 15-30 minutes if needed. Remove chicken and vegetables to a warm serving platter and take the onion, garlic, and lemon from the cavity. Make the sauce by pureeing in processor or blender all the garlic, 1 onion quarter, the pulp of 2 lemon quarters, and the released chicken juices. Taste for seasoning and adjust by adding more onion or more lemon.

Serves 3-4.

WILD AND WEEDY GREENS

In the garden of Eden, there were no weeds. The *dent-de-lion*, or dandelion, lay peaceably with lamb's quarters and lettuce, sourgrass with mustard and escarole. All leaves were young, tender, tame, and edible in the green and salad days of our first gardeners, who had no need of cooks.

In our own less perfect gardens, where leaves grow old and bitter and wild things war with tame, gardeners do need cooks to get the good out of plants that often suffer horticultural snobbery and culinary neglect. I learned my lesson from an herb garden so wet and shady it would grow only weeds and moss. Eventually I made peace with this garden by giving the weeds their head and by actually planting from seed an edible weed patch of dandelions, mustard, sorrel (the cultivated cousin of sourgrass), various kinds of cress, and a gang of chicories, endives, and escaroles.

I even learned to defend this garden by quoting from old cookbooks, which showed that many plants we now discard as weeds were once culled and cooked. Take lamb's quarters, better known as pigweed. While gardeners know that lamb's lettuce, also called corn salad, is an heirloom vegetable, cooks should know that lamb's quarters was once a valued edible green that is today an heirloom weed. Such "weeds" are still venerated by American Indians of the Southwest who have kept their knowledge of the wild.

Another such "weed" is purslane, supplanted in American gardens today by its showy and inedible cousin, portulaca. Purslane has been cultivated in Europe, however, since the Middle Ages. A recipe for "Pickled Pursland," found in *Martha Washington's Booke of Cookery* (1749), was common in American cookbooks until our own century. "Gather ye pursland," Martha says, "when it [is] stalkie & will snap when you break it. boyle it in a kettle of fayre water without any salt, & when it is tender, make a pickle of salt & water, as you doe for other pickles. & when it is cold, make it pretty sharp with vinegar & cover it as you did ye other prementioned pickles." The leaves of purslane are thick and faintly sour and the stems are pink, so that the plant is as decorative as it is piquant.

Then there is the Mustard family, which fills our salad bowls with mustard greens, nasturtiums, and cress, and the Composite family, which gives us dandelions and chicories. Until the last century nobody bothered to cultivate watercress because it grew wild by every pond. Dandelions and chicories, on the other hand, have long been cultivated in Europe, where the leaves are used in salads and are cooked as greens, and the roots are ground as a substitute for coffee.

All of these weedy plants are bitter, and since "bitter" is one of our four primary taste sensations (sweet, sour, bitter, and salty) some degree of bitterness has its own special appeal. Cultivated plants are less bitter than wild ones, young ones less bitter than old. Cooking not only tenderizes tough leaves and stalks but also tempers their strength. The first point with greens is that one kind of bitter leaf can substitute for another, and the more kinds mixed together, the better. The second point is that the "bitter" can be soothed by oil and vinegar, complemented by ham or bacon, accented by onion and garlic, moderated by eggs and cheese.

I confess that my weed patch turned me into an addict of bitter leaves, raw or cooked, and served hot, warm, or cold. Fortunately the addiction is common wherever people live close to the land. Americans think of the South as the home of cooked greens, so I've adapted a recipe from a Virginian, Stringfellow Barr, who wrote with Stella Standard *The Kitchen Garden Book* (1956). The Chinese think of greens, alone or in combination with other foods, in stir-fried woks. French and Italians think of greens civilized by cheese, eggs, and cream. And the English think of pickled purslane. While few gardeners would say, "Glory be to God for weedy things," cooks may yet find in edible weeds one way of regaining a weedless paradise.

Greens with Ham, Orange, and Mint

1 onion, chopped fine
1 tablespoon ham or bacon fat
1½ pounds greens, such as mustard, dandelion,
    curly endive, escarole, or chard
1 cup diced cooked ham or bacon
¼ cup chopped mint leaves
1 egg yolk
¼ cup orange juice
1 navel orange, peeled and segmented

Sauté onion in fat in a large pot. Wash greens and chop them. Mix them with ham and mint and add them to the pot. Cover and steam 10–20 minutes, or until greens are wilted. Drain well. Beat egg yolk with juice and pour over the greens. Arrange orange segments on top.
    Serves 4.

Chinese Stir-Fried Mustard Greens

1 teaspoon minced fresh ginger root
1 clove garlic, minced
2 scallions, chopped
1/4 teaspoon freshly ground black pepper
1 tablespoon peanut oil
1 1/2 pounds young mustard greens (or other greens)
1 tablespoon dark soy sauce
1/2 tablespoon wine vinegar
1 tablespoon sesame oil

Sauté ginger, garlic, scallions, and pepper in hot oil for half a minute. Add greens, chopped in 3-inch lengths, and stir-fry about 2 minutes, or until greens are wilted. Mix together soy sauce, vinegar, and sesame oil and pour over the greens. Good hot or cold.
Serves 4.

Pickled Purslane Salad

1/2 pound purslane
1 teaspoon sea salt
4 hard-cooked eggs
4 tomatoes
1/3 cup olive oil
1 tablespoon wine vinegar
Black pepper to taste

Wash purslane well. Chop leaves and stems together, sprinkle with salt, and let sit 24 hours. Slice or chop the eggs and tomatoes; add purslane. Mix the oil with vinegar and pepper and pour over the salad.
Serves 2–4.

Greens with Polenta

1 teaspoon salt
1½ cups cornmeal
5 cups water
4 slices bacon
2 tablespoons olive oil
2 cloves garlic, mashed
1 pound mixed greens, such as dandelion,
    mustard, chard, or spinach
salt and pepper to taste
¼ pound Romano Locatelli cheese
½ pound Fontina cheese

Mix salt with cornmeal in the top of a double boiler.
Bring water to a boil separately, then stir 2 cups of the
water slowly into the meal, stirring well. Add remaining
water, stir well, cover, and set the top in the bottom of
the boiler with at least 2 inches of water in it. Cook the
cornmeal about 20 minutes, stirring occasionally.

Cut the bacon in small pieces, fry until crisp, and set
aside. Add 1 tablespoon of the olive oil, the garlic, and the
well-washed greens. Season, cover with a tight lid, and
steam the greens until wilted, about 5 minutes. Drain
them (reserve liquid for another purpose such as soup)
and chop well, by food processor or by hand.

Grate the cheeses separately. Stir the Romano into
the polenta. Butter a standard loaf pan and fill it with a
layer of polenta, topped with a layer of greens, bacon, and
Fontina. Repeat and end with a layer of polenta. Sprinkle
the top with a little Fontina and the remaining olive oil.
Bake at 450° for 15 minutes to brown the top. Let sit 10
minutes before cutting in slices.

Serves 6–8.

July

July

NO–STRING BEANS

Green Bean Salad with Walnuts

French Beans the French Way

Green Beans with Yoghurt and Rice (*Fistuquia*)

Italian Beans with Pesto

BARBECUING FISH

Minted Bluefish

Indian-Smoked Salmon

Chinese-Smoked Bass

Barbecued Tuna Steaks

BLUEBERRIES:
"A MOST EXCELLENT SUMMER DISH"

Blueberry Bluefish

Blueberry Summer Pudding

Dried Blueberries with Kasha

Blueberry-Cherry Compote

Blueberry Sour Cream Cake

NO-STRING BEANS

Our great-grandmothers called them "French" beans because that's what the English called them. The French called them "Aztec" beans, turning the Aztec word *ayacotl* into *haricot* to distinguish these canoe-shaped beans from the only bean Europe had ever known before the discovery of America, the broad or fava bean. Amazingly, all the world's beans, except for the broad bean, originated in the New World. The green beans that we eat pod and all when they are young were cultivated 7,000 years ago in Mexico, so by rights we should call them "Mexican" beans.

My grandmother called them "string" or "snap" beans. From her I learned to top the stem end, zip the string down one side of the furry pod, nip off the tail, zip the string up the other side, then snap the bean in two. Two strings and one snap per bean, while we sat on the porch, the bean bowl between us, listening to "Vic and Sade." My children learned to string beans while watching "Leave It to Beaver," but by then we were down to one string and no snap because we served them whole. *Their* children, it seems, will never know the joys of stringing or snapping because today we pick beans younger and breed them to be stringless. Today we also import from France those costly fetal beans no bigger around than strings.

"French beans must be young and tender," Louis Eustache Ude admonished the English in vain in his 1828 *The French Cook*. "The fruiterers and green-grocers of this country sell them by the hundred when they are unfit to eat." They were unfit when they were old enough to string or snap, and English and American cooks of the nineteenth century advised their readers of the social consequences of unfit beans. Mary Randolph, in *The Virginia Housewife* (1824), stole the very words of *The Cook's Oracle* (1822), written by an English doctor, William Kitchiner, in discriminating unfit persons by their beans: "For common tables, they are split, and divided across; but those who are nice, do not use them at such a growth as to require splitting." Americans who were more inventive than nice devised the first cast-iron hand-powered bean splitters and slicers.

As the French developed the best varieties of garden bean, so they devised the best recipes for them. One of my favorites is a simple green bean salad served at room temperature and dressed with walnut oil and chopped walnuts. I sometimes vary it by mixing in other beans such as fresh limas, semi-dried white beans, or flageolets, and tender yellow wax beans.

The classic French way with young beans was to dress them with butter and cream. Hannah Glasse popularized this dish in England as a "ragoo" of beans, which Eliza Acton a century later called "An Excellent Receipt for French Beans à la Francaise" in her 1861 *Modern Cookery*, and the American Eliza Leslie, in her 1852 *New Receipts for Cooking*, called them "Stewed Beans (*French Way*)." Today we've become so accustomed to eating our beans so plain and nearly raw that this French sauce of cream and lemon, thickened by egg, seems like a startling innovation.

The green beans we call "Italian" are somewhat broader and flatter than the "French" ones, and they stand up well to a hearty dressing of pesto sauce in summertime, when basil inundates the garden and the cook. Pestoed beans are as delicious hot as cold, and you can turn a salad into a meal by adding sliced boiled potatoes, red onions, tomatoes, and chunks of mozzarella.

For more exotic Mediterranean fare, the Middle East offers a sauce of garlic and mint, instead of basil, to invigorate a cooling mixture of green beans, rice, and yoghurt. Paula Wolfert, in her 1985 *Mediterranean Cooking*, calls this dish *fistuquia.*

My grandmother would have been offended by beans too young to snap or string, and she would have boiled them for no less time than it took to reduce the accompanying lamb or beef to strings—at least 2 to 3 hours. Today we prefer to steam our tenderest baby beans for a mere 3 to 5 minutes or to boil them in their youthful prime for 10 to 15 minutes. To 3 quarts of water add 1½ tablespoons salt per pound of beans, drain the beans quickly, and splash them with cold water to retain their crisp texture and vivid green. My grandmother was not into crisp and vivid. She would have thought such beans as barbaric as the Aztecs and as decadent as the French, and she would have wondered where all the strings had gone, along with Vic and Sade.

Green Bean Salad with Walnuts

2 pounds fresh green beans
⅓ cup walnut oil
2 tablespoons lemon juice
  (or 1 tablespoon balsamic vinegar)
salt and pepper to taste
½ cup chopped walnuts

Parboil the beans, drain, and cool. Mix oil, lemon juice, salt, and pepper, and pour dressing over the beans. Sprinkle top with the walnuts.

Serves 4–6.

French Beans the French Way

1½ pounds fresh green beans
4-5 green onions, tops included, chopped
3 tablespoons butter
2 teaspoons flour
1 large egg yolk
1½ cups heavy cream
juice of 1 lemon
salt and pepper to taste
2 tablespoons fresh herbs, such as chervil,
    chopped, for garnish

Parboil the beans 5-15 minutes (depending on size
and age) in salted boiling water. Drain and splash with
cold water. Soften the onions in butter in a skillet, add
flour, and cook 2-3 minutes. Stir egg yolk into the cream,
whisk into the butter and flour, season to taste with
lemon juice, salt, and pepper, and let thicken slightly.
Add the beans, mix well, and serve. Garnish with chopped
herbs.
    Serves 4.

Green Beans with Yoghurt and Rice
(Fistuquia)

1 pound fresh green beans, cut in 1-inch lengths
1 whole egg
1 tablespoon cornstarch
2 cups yoghurt
1 cup cooked white rice

FOR THE TAKLIA SAUCE:
1 teaspoon minced garlic
1 tablespoon olive oil
2 tablespoons chopped fresh mint

Parboil the beans and drain. In a saucepan mix the egg into the cornstarch and beat mixture into the yoghurt. Bring mixture to a simmer and stir constantly until thick. Mix into the beans and rice. Make the sauce by sautéing the garlic in the oil 1 minute. Add mint and garnish beans and rice with the mixture.
Serves 4–6.

Italian Beans with Pesto

2 pounds fresh green beans
1/4 cup olive oil
1/4 teaspoon salt
1 large clove garlic, mashed
1 cup packed basil leaves
1/4 cup parsley leaves
2 tablespoons pine nuts
1/4 cup Parmesan cheese, grated

Parboil the beans and drain. Make a pesto sauce by putting oil, salt, garlic, basil, parsley, and nuts in a blender and pureeing them. Add cheese and blend again. Dilute as needed with more oil or a little hot water. Toss sauce with the beans and serve at room temperature.
Serves 4–6.

BARBECUING FISH

When Columbus discovered the West Indies, he found the natives grilling food over an open pit or campfire on a platform of sticks they called *barbacao*. That was how they cooked their fish, fowl, meat, and sometimes even people, using a method that combined roasting with smoking. Long before Europeans discovered America's Northwest coast, Indians there had developed smoking to a high art, building smokehouses of cedar that flavored salmon the way charred oak flavors bourbon.

I've discovered only recently how easy it is to reproduce these smoky tastes in my backyard grill and even my indoor skillet, without having to buy specialized equipment. You can buy inexpensive grills that are also smokers, but you don't have to. You do have to buy or acquire bunches of dried herbs or some flavorful wood-chips, such as alder, hickory, cherry, apple, or other fruit woods—or even the trendy mesquite—to add to your glowing charcoal. If your grill lacks a hood, you can improvise one with heavy-duty aluminum foil or a metal washtub, or whatever you can make fit.

If you're cooking indoors, you can produce a flavored smoke, as the Chinese learned to do in woodless China, by using burnt sugar, tea leaves, and rice placed in a foil-lined wok or a heavy cast-iron skillet covered with a foil-lined lid. If you like the effect of charred or crisped skin, you can broil the fish rapidly on both sides before smoking; you can char the skin in an ungreased cast-iron skillet preheated until it is almost white hot (about 10 minutes), or you can do what the Chinese do and deep-fry the fish after smoking.

Nothing is more delicious when marinated than the common Eastern bluefish, once so abundant that an 1870 reporter warned New Jersey of an invasion of blues: "Fish lie in creeks, ponds, etc., along the meadows two feet deep, so that one can take a common fork and pitch them into a boat or throw them on the bank." Here I've suggested a simple marinade of lime juice, flavored with fresh garden mint, but of course other fresh herbs will do as well. With a whole fish it's easiest to grill it in the marinade in a foil packet, which works like a mini-oven. With bluefish fillets, you can first marinate and then grill them directly, skin-side down, on a well-oiled grill.

Marinades were once made of salt or vinegar to help preserve flesh to be smoked, but we now use them largely for flavor. A dry cure of salt, sugar, and spices forms a brine as the salt draws out moisture from the flesh, and the brine, in turn, flavors it. Northwestern Indians today still dry-cure and double-smoke sides of salmon until they are so dry they can be stacked in a cupboard. To prepare a side of salmon for eating, they will first heat it and then dip it in a sauce of oil or butter, flavored with acid or one of many wild berries. James G. Swan, writing of the Washington Territory in 1857, found Indians collecting the wild salmon berry because it was "beneficial to counteract any ill effects that might be occasioned by inordinate eating of the rich salmon." In my own inordinate eating, I've found that a sauce of strawberries, raspberries, or blackberries, soured with a little fruit vinegar, is beneficial.

One of my favorite summer barbecues is meaty-fleshed tuna, marinated in soy, sherry, and ginger and served with a hot-pepper tofu mayonnaise. Tuna must be grilled quickly since the meat dries out badly if overcooked. Of course you can grill tuna under an oven broiler as well, if you can stand the heat on the kind of summer's day that tends to barbecue people as well as fish.

Minted Bluefish

rind and juice of 4 limes
2 cloves garlic, minced
¼ cup olive oil
2 green onions, tops included, chopped
1 cup packed fresh mint leaves, chopped
black and cayenne pepper to taste
1 whole bluefish, 4-6 pounds (or 2 pounds fillets)

Remove rind from the limes, chop fine, and set aside. Juice the limes and put juice in a blender with the garlic, oil, onion, half of the mint leaves, and the peppers. Put the fish in the blended marinade at room temperature for 1-2 hours. Place fish and marinade in a large square of heavy-duty foil and wrap it tightly so that you can turn the fish on the grill. Grill about 40 minutes, turning the fish halfway through. When ready to serve, sprinkle fish with remaining mint and the reserved lime rind.
Serves 4.

Indian-Smoked Salmon

½ cup kosher or sea salt
¼ cup brown sugar
1 teaspoon black pepper
¼ teaspoon each allspice and mace

2 pounds salmon fillets
¼ pound (1 stick) butter, melted
1 cup strawberries
1 tablespoon balsamic or fruit vinegar

Mix the salt, sugar, and spices and rub them into both sides of the salmon. Put the salmon in a plastic bag and refrigerate overnight. Rinse it well and dry on a rack for an hour before grilling. When your charcoal is ready, add a layer of wet hardwood chips. Put fish on the highest rack above the coals and cover tightly. Smoke as slowly as possible, 30–45 minutes (depending on thickness of fish and heat of coals). Put the butter, berries, and vinegar in a blender and liquefy. Adjust sourness and sweetness of the sauce with more vinegar or a little honey.
Serves 4.

Chinese-Smoked Bass

1 whole bass, 4–6 pounds
1 tablespoon salt
1 tablespoon powdered Szechuan peppercorns
3 tablespoons fresh ginger root, minced
3 green onions, chopped
½ cup brown sugar
½ cup Chinese black tea leaves
1 cup uncooked brown rice

Score bass on both sides, making cuts 2 inches apart. Warm the salt and pepper in a hot skillet, then mix with the ginger and onions and rub the mixture into the bass inside and out. Wrap in plastic wrap and refrigerate 2–6 hours. Line a wok or cast-iron skillet with heavy-duty foil. Mix sugar, tea leaves, and rice in the center of the foil.

Unwrap the fish and place it on a greased cake rack on top of the sugar mixture in the wok. Line a wok cover or skillet lid with a layer of foil that will extend a few inches below the rim of the lid to help seal it. Cover the wok and cook over medium heat 20 minutes. Turn off the heat and let the fish smoke, covered, for 20 minutes more. Serve hot or at room temperature.

Serves 4.

Barbecued Tuna Steaks

2 pounds tuna steaks, 1 inch thick
1/4 cup soy sauce
1/4 cup peanut oil
1 tablespoon sesame oil
1 clove garlic, mashed
1 tablespoon fresh ginger root, minced
1 small hot chili pepper, minced
1/2 cup dry sherry
1 teaspoon black pepper
3/4 pound (1 1/3 cups) tofu, drained

Marinate tuna 4–8 hours in a marinade made from all the listed ingredients except the tofu. Drain the steaks, reserve the marinade, and grill the steaks quickly over charcoal or hardwood chips, or under a broiler, turning once to sear each side. Make a mayonnaise by putting the marinade and tofu in a blender and pureeing until smooth. Serve sauce with the fish.

Serves 4.

BLUEBERRIES: "A MOST EXCELLENT SUMMER DISH"

"Sky-coloured billberries" was how John Josselyn in *New England's Rarities Discovered* (1672) described the wild berries he found in the New World. They were bluer than the bilberries or whortleberries of his native England. "The Indians dry them in the Sun and sell them to the English by the Bushell," he explained. The English colonists used bushels of the dried berries in place of traditional currants in their puddings, gruels, and fruitcakes, and in summertime they doused fresh berries in sweetened spiced milk or sherry for "a most excellent Summer Dish."

Wild berries are often wildly named. In the west country of England the bilberry, for which Josselyn mistook our native blueberry, was also called whortleberry or hurtleberry for its color, which reminded some of "hurted" or bruised flesh. In America the names hurtleberry and whortleberry were conflated into "huckleberry," another wild blue that is close kin to the true blueberry of the Vaccinium family. Huckleberry later came to personify American wildness and the name stuck. Imagine how different the course of American literature and lives if Twain had written *The Adventures of Whortleberry Finn.*

It was the blueberry, however, and not the huckleberry that botanists hybridized at the beginning of this century to produce many cultivated varieties of highbush berry, with names like Earliblue, Late Blue, Blueray, and Bluetta. And it was the cultivated blueberry that the New World sent to the Old in 1946 in the form of eight highbush plants to be nurtured in Dorset, England, formerly the heart of whortleberry country. So new still are these Yankee berries to English greengrocers that boxes of Dorset blueberries are accompanied with recipes printed in "bilberry-purple ink," as Jane Grigson notes in her 1985 *British Cookery*, wherein she suggests using blueberries in that quintessentially English dish, Summer Pudding.

The first English colonists put blueberries in their traditional puddings of fruit and dough, but as the English language turned American, so did pudding names. "Grunt," "buckle," and "slump" reveal the self-mockery of Yankee humor. "Buckle" or "slump" usually referred to fruit covered with biscuit dough and baked in the oven. "Grunt" was the same fruit and dough steamed in a pudding mold. Typical of more high-toned recipes for blueberries were the batter breads and cakes provided by Eliza Leslie in her 1837 *Directions for Cookery*. Her "Huckleberry Cake" is really an early form of blueberry muffin, spiced with molasses, cinnamon, and cloves, and poured "in a buttered pan, or into little tins." Maria Parloa, in her 1872 *Appledore Cook Book*, used blueberries for an English trifle she called "Appledore Pudding," layering blueberries with stale cake splashed with wine and topped with meringue.

In the recipes here, I've recalled English tradition in a blueberry summer pudding, a blueberry sour cream cake (related to Miss Eliza's huckleberry cake), and in a blueberry-cherry compote, which makes a good nonsoggy filling for a prebaked tart shell. I do hate gummy crusts or cornstarch thickeners and both nasties can be avoided by using fresh fruit combined with fruit jam.

I've also turned back to the Indian tradition of drying berries, which helps today's cultivated blueberry recapture some of the intensity of its wild relative. Drying berries is easy. Just spread a single layer of berries on a number of baking sheets and put them in a sunny spot for 4 or 5 days, or bake them in a very low oven (150°) for 4 or 5 hours. Berries fully dried will keep indefinitely in a plastic bag or glass jar. Dried berries plump up in any liquid, so they are particularly good with kasha, wild rice, or other grains.

Finally, I've executed a modest culinary pun by baking bluefish in a blueberry sauce, but it's sanctioned by the Indian tradition of flavoring fish and game with wild berries of all kinds. The sweetness of blueberries is both countered and accented by lemon or vinegar in a fish sauce. With a dash of port or crème de cassis, blueberries, like cranberries, make an excellent sauce for any dark meat such as game, duck, or lamb.

"Real sky-blue," Robert Frost called the wild berries of New Hampshire, which absorbed the smoke of cleared and burned woods in the bloom of their skins and the flavor of their flesh. "It must be on charcoal they fatten their fruit," Frost writes. "I taste in them sometimes the flavour of soot." One way to discover New England's rarities today is to do as the Indians did. Make an excellent summer dish by garnishing grilled fish and meats with sky-colored, soot-flavored blueberries.

Blueberry Bluefish

salt and pepper to taste
4 bluefish fillets, 1/4–1/2 pound each
1 cup blueberries
1 cup dry white wine
1 tablespoon chopped green onion
1/4 cup wine (or blueberry) vinegar
1/2 pound (2 sticks) butter
mint leaves for garnish (optional)

Salt and pepper the fish fillets on both sides and put in a buttered baking dish. Puree the blueberries, wine, onion, and vinegar and pour over the fish. Bake at 350° about 8 minutes (or until barely fork tender). Remove fillets to a warm platter. In a saucepan, reduce sauce to about a cup, lower heat, and beat in the butter, a table-spoon at a time, until the sauce thickens and smooths out. Pour over fish and garnish with a sprig or two of mint.

Serves 4.

Blueberry Summer Pudding

12 or more ½-inch-thick slices
   stale white bread
1 quart blueberries
½ cup red or black currants (optional)
½ cup sugar
2-3 tablespoons Grand Marnier (optional)
1 cup heavy cream, whipped

Cut crusts from the bread and trim the slices so that you can completely line (without any gaps) a glass or ceramic bowl, to use as a mold. Heat the blueberries and currants with the sugar and liqueur until juice begins to ooze. Pack the fruit into the bread-lined mold and reserve some of the juice. Cover the fruit with a layer of bread and pour the juice over it. Cover the top layer of bread with a plate and a heavy can or two (so that the fruit will soak into the bread). Refrigerate for 24 hours and unmold just before serving. Serve with lots of whipped cream.

Serves 4-6.

Dried Blueberries with Kasha

1 cup kasha, or buckwheat groats
1 egg, beaten
2 cups boiling chicken broth
½ cup dried blueberries
1 ounce dried mushrooms, soaked in
  ½ cup hot water
salt and pepper to taste
4 tablespoons (½ stick) butter

Heat a heavy skillet, add the kasha and the beaten egg, and stir vigorously with a fork until every grain is coated and distinct. Add the chicken broth, dried blueberries, mushrooms, and seasonings, cover the pan, and steam the kasha over low heat for 30 minutes. Stir in the butter.
Serves 4.

Blueberry-Cherry Compote

1 cup cherry preserves or blueberry jam
¼-½ cup port
2 cups blueberries
2 cups Bing cherries, pitted
rind of 1 orange, grated

Melt preserves in a pan with the port and pour over the fresh fruit, mixed with the orange rind. (If too sweet, add a little lemon juice or orange juice.) To serve hot bring to a simmer just before serving. To serve cold chill until needed.
Serves 4-8.

Blueberry Sour Cream Cake

3 cups blueberries
2 cups all-purpose flour
¼ pound (1 stick) butter
1½ cups sugar
2 eggs, beaten
1 cup sour cream
rind of 1 lemon, grated
1 tablespoon baking powder
1 tablespoon each cinnamon and cloves, mixed
½ teaspoon salt
powdered sugar

Coat berries with ⅓ cup flour and reserve. Cream butter and sugar, beat in the eggs, and blend in the sour cream and lemon rind. Mix remaining flour with baking powder and seasonings and stir into the egg batter. Fold in the blueberries. Pour batter into a well-buttered Bundt pan and bake at 350° for 1-1½ hours, or until a toothpick comes out clean. Cool 10 minutes in the pan, then turn onto cake rack. When cake is cool, sprinkle top with powdered sugar.

Serves 8-12.

August

August

THE SWEETEST CORN OF ALL

Green Corn Griddle Cakes

Sweet Corn and Cucumber Soup

Italian Corn Salad

Baked Corn with Onions

Green Corn and Blueberry Pudding

"AND CALLED IT MACARONI"

Macaroni Calico Salad

Tanu

Newlywed Macaroni and Cheese

Apple Butter Noodle Pudding

SUN-SOAKED SUMMER FRUITS

Gooseberry Fool

Raspberries in Raspberry Cream

Sour Cherry Tart

Almond Crust

Peaches in Brandied Peach Marmalade

THE SWEETEST CORN
OF ALL

One of my favorite forms of American humor is the tall
tale or exaggeration postcard, a spoofery wildly popular
in the early 1900s, when photographers faked such anoma-
lies as fur-bearing trout, jackalopes (jack rabbits with
antelope antlers), and elephantine fruits and vegetables.
I have a card from 1909 that shows a farmer balancing
himself on a single ear of corn so big that it fills his
horse-drawn wagon. The farmer is chopping off corn kernels with a pickax before he takes his saw to the cob. The
legend reads, "How We Do Things at Wichita, Kans."

In 1909 that card must have given the recipient, a
Miss Hilda Gardner of Lincoln, Nebraska, a hearty laugh.
Today it seems a prevision of what actually happened to
corn in this country, a success story beyond the dreams
of the American corn grower and of the American corn
eater, both of whom fantasized about endless wagons of
colossal corn. Shortly after this card was sent, Henry
Wallace began to experiment with hybrids that would
eventually fulfill fantasies of corn as high as an elephant's
eye and as sweet as Sweet Sue or Kandy Korn, to name
but two recent hybrids.

Where hungry lovers of fresh corn were once limited
to the green youth of indigenous types like dent and flint,
bred for meal and fodder, nowadays they can indulge all
summer long in corn bred for sweetness and creaminess.

And where Labor Day once meant the end of the affair, now corn lovers can feast on through the fall, savoring the ripeness of late bloomers.

In August, however, corn is at its sweetest, when corn lovers in their madness attack wagonloads of tightly wrapped green-husked cobs and dive into lakes of butter. With cornucopias of corn, now is the time to cut kernels from the cob and to squeeze out their milky interiors so that they may lend their sweetening and thickening powers to companionate foods.

For the Zunis of the American Southwest, the ripening of new corn in the fields was an occasion for ceremony. They celebrated the return of the lost corn maidens in a ceremony they called the "Meeting of the Children," where the woman elected to be corn matron would address a few of the most perfect ears of corn newly plucked from their stalks, "My children, how be ye these many days?" and a group of women would answer in the voices of the new corn, "Happily, our old ones, happily."

From Indians west and east, colonists happily learned how to cut kernels from new corn to make succotash with new beans and other vegetables. They also learned how to grate green corn and add it to their own recipes for soups, puddings, fritters, and griddle cakes. For a couple of centuries, green corn was a traditional ingredient for thickening and flavoring a custard of milk and eggs to make a pudding or, if the eggs were separated, a soufflé. In my recipe here, I've turned the pudding into a dessert soufflé by adding blueberries for accent and color.

New Englanders often added fresh corn to their seafood and potato chowders, or made chowders of corn alone. Here I've added corn to a light cucumber soup, good cold on a hot, hot day. In another recipe I've twinned corn with onions to double their sweetness in a simple baked dish flavored with curry. To turn this into a one-dish meal, you could add some haddock or cod.

In pursuit of fresh corn recipes, I came on *The Corn Cook Book* of 1918, labeled "War Edition" and designed to "Save the Wheat" for ourselves and our Allies by encouraging us to eat more corn. The author, Elizabeth O. Hiller, found some fifty-one ways to use green corn, as she calls it, in omelets, hashes, croquettes, timbales, fritters, waffles, griddle cakes, and all manner of cornmeal muffins, cakes, and breads. Her pancake batter of delicate fresh corn can't be beat. "Corn," Mrs. Hiller declares, "is the American Indian's greatest gift to civilization." To some that might seem an exaggeration, but to lovers of sweet fresh corn its truth is self-evident.

Green Corn Griddle Cakes

1 cup half-and-half or buttermilk
2 tablespoons butter, melted
2 eggs
1 cup unbleached flour
1 teaspoon salt
1 tablespoon sugar
2 teaspoons baking powder
2 cups fresh corn kernels*

In a blender or processor, or by hand, mix together until smooth all the ingredients but the corn kernels. Stir kernels into the batter and ladle ¼ cup at a time onto a

Note on how to remove corn kernels from cob: Hold cob vertically over a wide-mouthed shallow bowl or pan. Cut kernels straight down, top to bottom, with a sharp knife. Turn knife over and with its dull side scrape the cob down on all sides to get all the "milk." If you want more creaminess than crunch, score the kernels first, down the middle of each row, before cutting them off.

greased hot griddle or skillet. Flip cakes over with a spatula when their tops are puffed and their edges dry.

Yields 8-12 cakes.

Sweet Corn and Cucumber Soup

2 green onions, chopped, with tops
2 tablespoons butter
4 cups peeled and sliced cucumbers
6 cups chicken broth
2 cups fresh corn kernels
1 cup yoghurt
salt and pepper to taste
Garnish: ¼ cup chives

Lightly sauté onions in the butter, add cucumbers and the chicken broth, and simmer 15 minutes. Add all but ½ cup corn and simmer 5 more minutes. Puree the mixture in a blender, processor, or food mill. Add up to 1 cup of yoghurt, depending on thickness wanted. Season with salt and pepper, and serve hot or cold. Sprinkle remaining corn kernels and chopped chives on top of each bowl of soup.

Serves 6-8.

Italian Corn Salad

2 cups fresh corn kernels
3 large tomatoes, sliced thin
1/4 pound mozzarella, cut in strips
1 small bunch basil
1/3 cup olive oil
1 1/2 tablespoons vinegar
salt and pepper to taste

Heap uncooked corn kernels in center of a salad platter. Encircle with overlapping slices of tomato. Arrange mozzarella strips like spokes of a wheel radiating from the corn. Make an outside border of basil leaves. Beat oil, vinegar, and seasonings together, and pour over the whole.
Serves 4.

Baked Corn with Onions

4 cups fresh corn kernels
2 cups thinly sliced onions
1 teaspoon curry powder
salt and pepper to taste
1/4 pound (1 stick) butter
1/2 cup heavy cream

Alternate corn and onions in layers in a buttered baking dish. Sprinkle with curry powder and salt and pepper. Cut butter in slices over the top. Pour on cream. Bake at 375° for 35-45 minutes, or until top is browned.
Serves 4-6.

Green Corn and Blueberry Pudding

3 cups fresh corn kernels
1½ cups blueberries
3 tablespoons cornstarch
⅓ to ½ cup sugar
1 teaspoon salt
⅛ teaspoon mace or nutmeg
4 eggs, separated
1 cup heavy cream
4 tablespoons butter, melted

In a bowl toss corn and blueberries with cornstarch, sugar, salt, and mace mixed together. Beat the 4 egg yolks into the cream and pour over the corn mixture. Stir in the butter. Beat egg whites until stiff and fold into the mixture. Pour into a buttered (2 quart) baking dish and bake at 350° for 30–45 minutes.

Serves 4–6.

"AND CALLED IT MACARONI"

When Yankee Doodle went to London, riding on a pony, he was no doubt a yokel, but he was not so dumb as to mistake a feather for a piece of pasta. When he stuck a feather in his cap and called it "macaroni," he was merely aping a set of London dandies who in turn had affected the fashions of the Bourbon court at Naples. In the 1760s the Neapolitan court had made all things Italian so very fashionable that trend-setting Londoners had formed a club and named it after Naples' most famous dish. Yankee Doodle, in his trendy headwear, simply wanted to join the club.

Maccheroni, as the Italians spelled it, was a generic term for any flour-and-water paste, whether rolled flat like lasagne, shaped into long hollow tubes like cannelloni, or squeezed into thin strands like spaghetti. Housewives of ancient Rome were rolling out these floury pastes several centuries before Marco Polo discovered the Chinese rolling such pastes for their egg rolls, noodles, and wontons.

In Europe, *maccheroni* generally was used as a wrapper to enclose minced and spiced stuffings of meat, cheese, fruit, and vegetables. Unstuffed pasta did not become a major dish until the culinary innovations of the Bourbon chef, the great Corrado, coincided with the invention of the first pasta machine. In the latter half of the eighteenth century, Naples and Genoa began to mass-produce in factories the *maccheroni* that had formerly been made only by hand.

Thomas Jefferson, always keen on continental fashion, sent his protégé, William Short, to Naples in 1789 to bring back a "macaroni mould" for the Monticello kitchen. Short wrote to Jefferson that he had found a mold, but that it was "of a smaller diameter than that used at the manufactories of maccaroni." Evidently Short had found a spaghetti mold, but he hastened to add that thin tubes were more fashionable than large ones. "I went to see them made," he explained. "I observed that the maccaroni most esteemed at Naples was smaller than that generally seen at Paris." This new macaroni hastened the use of a newfangled table instrument, the three-pronged fork, which, according to Giuliano Bugialli in *The Fine Art of Italian Cooking* (1978), the Italians invented in order to eat spaghetti in a more refined manner than could be managed with the hands.

Jefferson called any form of flour-and-water noodles "macaroni" in his receipt book at Monticello. In his recipe for "Noodles to Thicken the Soup," he explains, "If you mean to dress them as macaroni, drop them in boiling water, cover fifteen minutes and drain." What was new was dressing the pasta with butter and cheese to serve as a course in itself.

Medieval Englanders had called an earlier prototype of macaroni "macrows," which was really a kind of dumpling for thickening soup. It was easy to roll "macrows" flat into "noodles," but harder to make them round like tubes. "Take some good flour and mix with water and make a paste a little thicker than that of lasagna, and wrap it around a stick," instructs Maestro Martino, a macaroni maker in the fifteenth century. "Then throw away the stick and cut the paste the width of the little finger."

In early nineteenth-century American cookbooks, "To Dress Macaroni" meant to dress homemade noodles in the Italian style. "Allow half a pound of butter to a pound of macaroni and half a pound of cheese," writes Miss Eliza Leslie in 1837. The cheese, of course, was Parmesan. Carolina Rutledge, in her 1847 *Carolina Housewife,* adds an Anglo-French twist with a white sauce, "à la Sauce Blanche," to be layered with the macaroni and Parmesan "until the dish is filled." Such is the origin of the macaroni-and-cheese casseroles of my childhood, with the significant substitution of Kraft Velveeta for Italian Parmesan.

One of the first recipes I wrote as a newlywed, in a notebook I now find both comic and pathetic, was for macaroni and cheese. I've printed it here verbatim because I can't improve on its simplicity. Another childhood favorite, which I did not set down in my notebook, is the macaroni salad of church suppers and Fourth of July picnics. Printed recipes for it were scarce until the 1950s, perhaps because the recipes were so easy they could be passed by word of mouth. I recently came on a nice version that Irma Rombauer, in her 1964 *Joy of Cooking,* calls "Calico Salad." The name aptly describes a combination of red and green summer vegetables with white macaroni.

Another, more unusual cold macaroni dish comes from an exotic recipe dating back to the Saracen conquest of Sicily in the ninth century. This is a molded loaf called "Tanu," still served today in Sicily at Easter. The loaf may originally have celebrated the departure of the heathen, but it retained a Saracen name and look, for it layers a large grooved pasta tube called *rigatoni* with cheese and parsley and spices it with a surprising cinnamon. Each slice forms a Moorish mosaic of white, yellow, and green. Out of fashion these days is the practice of dressing macaroni with sugar, cinnamon, and nutmeg and serving it with cream for dessert. Dessert macaroni was so popular at the turn of the century, however, that Lizzie Kander, in her 1915 *Settlement Cookbook,* gives three recipes for "Noodle Pudding," one of them an elaborate soufflé with citron, apples, and currants. I've adapted a plain but delicious one here, using apple butter and sour cream instead of Kander's plum butter, but you can use any good fruit preserve.

Today macaroni is no longer the generic term for Italian pasta. Today we distinguish "macaroni" from "rigatoni," "fettucini," "penne," "ravioli," "linguine," "tagliatelle," and "tortellini," to name but a few. Today, it seems, every modern Yankee Doodle has a Jeffersonian pasta machine in his kitchen, instead of a feather in his cap, to indicate that he is a member in good standing of the ever more fashionable pasta club.

Macaroni Calico Salad

2 cups cooked macaroni
¼ cup olive oil
1 tablespoon lemon juice or vinegar
1 cup raw diced zucchini
1 cup peeled, seeded, and chopped
    fresh tomatoes
3 green onions, chopped fine
1 cup each roasted and diced sweet red and
    green bell peppers
½ cup sliced stuffed green olives
1 cup minced parsley
1 cup yoghurt
1 teaspoon salt
½ teaspoon black pepper
⅛ teaspoon cayenne pepper
¼ cup chopped chives

Toss the macaroni in the oil and lemon juice while preparing the vegetables. Combine the vegetables, olives, and parsley with the macaroni, mix in the yoghurt, salt, and peppers, and taste for seasoning. Sprinkle top with chives. Cover and refrigerate at least an hour to blend flavors.

Serves 4-6.

Tanu

½ pound rigatoni
10 eggs, beaten
1 cup chopped Italian parsley
¼ pound Parmesan cheese, grated
½ teaspoon salt
1 teaspoon black pepper
½ teaspoon cinnamon
¼ pound salted ricotta (or Greek feta) cheese
¼ pound fresh ricotta

Boil the rigatoni in salted water about 8 minutes. It should be just *al dente.* Drain it well. Beat the eggs with the parsley, Parmesan, and seasonings. Line a standard bread pan (9 × 5 × 3) with well-oiled foil. Pour a thin layer of the egg mixture in the bottom of the pan and add a layer of rigatoni in even rows lengthwise (3 rows of 5 tubes). Grate the firm, salted ricotta (or crumble the feta) cheese and sprinkle half of it on the rigatoni. Pour on one-third of the egg mixture. Spread on half the fresh ricotta and cover with another layer of rigatoni. Repeat with the 2 cheeses and egg mixture. Cover with a final layer of rigatoni and the final third of the egg mix. Cover with a sheet of oiled foil. Place bread pan inside a larger pan and fill with an inch or two of boiling water. Bake at 325° for 1½ hours. Refrigerate until cold and unmold. Serve in thin slices.

Yields 1 loaf.

Newlywed Macaroni and Cheese

Cook: One 8-ounce package macaroni
Combine: 4 tablespoons butter, 3 tablespoons flour
Add to: 3 cups scalded milk
Let cook 20 minutes.
Add: 1½ cups sharp cheese, 1 teaspoon salt

Combine sauce with macaroni in baking dish. Sprinkle top with another ½ cup cheese and dot with butter. Bake in hot oven (400-500°) 15-20 minutes.
Serves 2.

Apple Butter Noodle Pudding

½ pound rigatoni or macaroni
2 tablespoons butter
1½ cups walnuts, grated
½ cup sugar
1 teaspoon cinnamon
¼ teaspoon nutmeg
1-pound jar of apple butter
1 cup sour cream

Boil pasta in lightly salted water until fork tender. Drain well. Mix with butter. Place half the pasta in a buttered baking dish. Mix together the nuts, sugar, cinnamon, and nutmeg, and sprinkle half the mixture over the pasta. Ladle on the apple butter and cover it with the sour cream. Layer with the remaining pasta and sprinkle top with the remaining nut mixture. Bake at 300° for 30-40 minutes. Serve hot or cold.
Serves 6-8.

SUN-SOAKED
SUMMER FRUITS

What is so frustrating as a day in August, when bushel baskets of apricots, cherries, peaches, and plums—all the sun-soaked fruits of summer—come ripe all at once and clamor to be eaten on the spot? There is only one solution to the fresh fruit problem and that is the sugar solution.

As salt preserves meat, sugar preserves fruit. After sugar became available in the eighteenth century to orders lower than the nobility, cookbooks devoted large sections to sweetmeats, or to the preservation of fruits and flowers by means of marmalades, conserves, pastes, candies, syrups, and jellies. Martha Washington's *Booke of Sweetmeats* in 1749 typically tells the cook how "To Preserve damsons other plums or Apricocks to keep all ye year in a quackeing Ielley."

Preserving whole fruits in a quaking jelly was only one way of halting nature's decay. Another way was to turn fruits into liquor, to make such dainties as peach shrub, plum brandy, or cherry ratafia. Yet another way was to turn fruit into "leather" by boiling sugared fruit to a paste that was then dried in sheets and cut in fancy shapes like lozenges. The simplest way was to "stove" fruit by coating it in syrup and drying it slowly in the oven or in the sun.

When gardening and cooking were twin branches of the same art, a "fresh" fruit dessert meant one prepared from fruit previously "stewed"

in a little sugar. "Always stew the fruit before placing it in a pie or a crust," warned Mrs. Seely in her *Cook Book* of 1902, because stewed fruit can be drained of its juice. Only later in the century did cooks resort to flour, cornstarch, or other nasty thickeners to absorb the juice of uncooked fruit piled into an uncooked crust.

The best way to thicken fruit juice is the traditional way of letting it thicken itself by heating it in small quantities (no more than a pound at a time) with enough sugar (but never more than a pound of sugar to a pound of fruit) to release the natural pectin that makes fruits jell. By allowing the pectin to work, you intensify their fruit flavor instead of diluting it. And you buy time, because the stewed or jellied fruit will keep until you are ready to fold it into a lovely custard or cream, a tart, a cake, or a pie.

In the recipes here, I've suggested folding stewed gooseberries into that time-honored whimsy the English call a "fool." The custard is the same as for a "trifle," but without the sherry and with "topped and tailed" berries (stem and blossom ends removed) mashed into a puree. I've also suggested folding fresh raspberry jam into crème fraîche scented with the heavenly raspberry liqueur *framboise* to glorify the luxury fruit that raspberries have become.

The lover of poached peaches can double his peach consumption by baking them in a peach marmalade flavored with brandy, honey, and the peach kernels traditionally used to lend their distinctive bitter-almond taste. I like to "poach" peaches by baking them because they keep their firmness that way.

The cherry pie lover (and who does not love a sour cherry pie?) can avoid the soggy crust problem by first baking a nut crust and then filling it with whole cherries preserved in a "quaking" plum jam. Because cherries are low in pectin, you need to combine them with a fruit high in pectin like plums, currants, or quince to make the cherry syrup jell.

You can vary the sweetness or tartness of any of these fruit purees, marmalades, jellies, and jams by balancing sugar with lime or lemon juice. Since the fruit itself will vary in sweetness depending on breed, weather, sap, and sun, let taste be your guide in finding what degree of sweetness pleases your palate. Provided, of course, that your palate is not already numb from eating on the spot all those clamoring baskets of apricots, cherries, peaches, and plums.

Gooseberry Fool

3/4 pound gooseberries (1 cup puree)
3/4 pound sugar, or to taste
1 tablespoon butter
1 cup half-and-half
3 egg yolks, beaten
1 cup heavy cream, whipped
1/4 teaspoon nutmeg or mace

Remove stem and blossom end of berries (scissors are easier than a knife) and put berries in a saucepan with the sugar and butter. Simmer, stirring, until the berries are soft enough to mash with a fork (about 15 minutes). Heat the half-and-half to the boiling point and pour slowly over the beaten egg yolks. Heat the egg mixture in the top of a double boiler, stirring constantly, until the custard thickens enough to coat the spoon. Cool, stir in the gooseberry puree, and chill. Before serving, spoon the whipped cream on top and sprinkle with nutmeg.

Serves 4-6.

Raspberries in Raspberry Cream

2 pints fresh raspberries
3/4–1 cup sugar
1 cup crème fraîche or heavy cream
2 tablespoons *framboise*

Combine half the berries with the sugar in a saucepan and simmer, stirring, until the juice thickens enough
to make a jellied blob when dropped from a spoon onto a
plate. Pour the jam into a jar and cool. Whip cream until
stiff; fold in 3 or 4 tablespoons of the jam and the *framboise*.
Put into the bottom of a glass bowl and cover with the
rest of the fresh raspberries.

Serves 4.

Sour Cherry Tart

1 pound sour cherries
1 pound (2 cups) sugar
juice of 1 lemon
6 redskinned plums
1 almond crust

Pit cherries, cover with sugar, and let stand overnight.
Bring fruit to a boil in a saucepan and simmer about 10
minutes. Remove cherries with slotted spoon and reserve.
To the syrup, add lemon juice and plums, cut in pieces,
but include skins and pits. Simmer about 30 minutes, or
until syrup begins to jell. Strain and pour

into a jar. Just before serving, fill prebaked tart shell with the cherries and spoon jelly over the top.

Serves 4–8.

Almond Crust

½ cup almonds, pulverized
1 cup flour
¼ teaspoon salt
3 tablespoons powdered sugar
6 tablespoons butter, chilled
¼ teaspoon vanilla extract
1 egg, beaten

Pulverize nuts in blender or processor. Combine with flour, salt, and sugar. Cut butter in cubes and work it into the flour quickly (by hand or processor), until butter is the size of peas. Beat vanilla into the egg and add to the flour mixture. Press dough together, wrap it in plastic wrap, and refrigerate overnight. With your fingertips, press the dough rapidly into the bottom and sides of a 9-inch pie plate and flute the top edge. Prick the bottom with a fork. Line the pie shell with foil and fill it with beans or rice to keep the shell from shrinking. Bake at 375° for 5–7 minutes, until dough is set. Remove foil, prick shell again, and continue baking until golden, 10–15 more minutes.

Yields one 9-inch pie shell.

Peaches in Brandied Peach Marmalade

8 large cling or freestone peaches
2 cups sugar
juice of 2 limes
2 tablespoons brandy
2 tablespoons honey (optional)

Blanch the peaches for 1 minute in boiling water to remove their skins. Halve them and remove pits. Smash the pits with a hammer and remove the skins of the inner kernels. Slice half the fruit into a saucepan and add sugar, half the lime juice, and the peach kernels. Simmer until fruit is translucent and the syrup thickened. Remove from heat and add remaining lime juice and brandy. Taste for sweetness and add honey if wanted. Leave marmalade chunky or puree it until smooth. Place remaining peaches in a baking pan, pour the marmalade over them, and cover the pan with foil. Bake at 250° for about 30 minutes. Serve warm or cold.

    Serves 4-8.

September

September

SEPTEMBER'S TOMATOES

Homemade Tomato Ketchup

Double-Red Tomato Sauce

Green Tomato Marmalade

THE WELL-BRED RABBIT

Venetian Rabbit

Grilled Rabbit with Fennel

Rabbit in Coconut Milk

Rabbit in Lemon, Garlic, and Thyme

THE PLEASURES OF PLUMMING

Plum-Barbecued Ribs

Orange-Glazed Plums

Walnut-Plum Tart

Fresh Plum Ice Cream

SEPTEMBER'S TOMATOES

In September, when the garden, the children, and even the bugs are drowning in a red tide of ripe, juicy, sun-hot tomatoes, we might remember January. In January we'll be beached high and dry in a desert of those pale pink polyester globes that simulate tomatoes in wintertime. In January it's too late to remember the grasshopper and the ant. As the poet says, "Provide, provide."

Provident Americans learned long ago from the English, those great processors and preservers of the world's goods, how to preserve tasty foods in the form of ketchups or catsups. English tea traders had learned the trick from the Malays, who provided both the sauce and the word "kechap." Originally the sauce was a type of brine or vinegar, based on soy, anchovies, mushrooms, or oysters, that became known variously in England as Harvey's or Worcestershire or H. P. Sauce.

In America, blessed or cursed, depending on your point of view, with an abundance of tomatoes from Mexico, tomatoes were substituted for mushrooms or oysters early in the nineteenth century. By 1824 the "love apple," once distrusted as both an aphrodisiac and a cancer-producing poison, appears as a major condiment in Mrs. Mary Randolph's *The Virginia Housewife* in the form of "Tomato Catsup," "Tomato Marmalade," and "Tomato Soy."

In contrast to ketchup today, however, nineteenth-century tomato ketchup was spicy with cinnamon and

cloves, hot with mustard, sour with vinegar, and sweet
with nothing at all. Not until the turn of the century,
when an enterprising preserver named Henry J. Heinz
put the first commercial tomato ketchup on tables from
Philadelphia to Singapore, did sugar become a major
ingredient of the pickled sauce.

For those who have known only the commercially
bottled product, a freshly made ketchup may come as a
revelation of how the natural sweetness and sourness of
the acidic fruit can be intensified and enlivened by spices
and aromatics. In the ketchup recipe here, I've added, to
Mrs. Randolph's mace and black pepper, Eliza Leslie's
wider spice range in her recipe for "Tomata Catchup" in
her *Directions for Cookery* (1837). I've also added a small
amount of sugar to make the sauce recognizable to today's
ketchup lovers, who might otherwise mistake it for a hot
tomato sauce like the Mexican *salsa picante*.

Ketchup traditionally should be smooth and so thick
that it doesn't pour but rather splats from a bottle struck
sharply with the heel of the hand. One advantage of homemade ketchup is that you can devise your own container
and avoid the common hazards of uncontrolled splatting.

Tomato ketchup, of course, is only an intensified tomato
puree, halfway between stewed tomatoes and tomato paste.
Sauces of other kinds will equally preserve the summer
sun of tomatoes, and now that we have freezers, putting
up tomatoes is not the arduous, hot, and steamy task it
was in the heyday of the sterilized Mason jar.

Tomato sauces can be thin, thick, crunchy, or smooth,
according to kind and preference. In the "Double-Red"
sauce here, I've added sweet red peppers for color,
sweetness, and crunch, since peppers hold their shape
even as tomatoes lose theirs. With a food processor you
can make the cooked sauce more or less chunky by puls-
ing the machine a few times. Without a processor you can

simply chop the vegetables before cooking them or put the sauce through the coarsest disk of a food mill. With a blender you can liquefy the vegetables to make a thick, smooth puree that is delicious with fish, chicken breasts, and veal chops.

Finally, when frost threatens, you can make good use of green tomatoes, those late unripe fruits, by preserving them as a piquant marmalade. Tomato marmalade should be as thick and chunky as a good orange marmalade. Like her ketchup, Mrs. Randolph's tomato marmalade is a hot and spicy unsweetened conserve. But as the century progressed, so did the sweetening. The marmalade here balances the sweetness of sugar with the sourness of vinegar, citron, and the green tomatoes themselves. This is good as a relish for meats, but I also like eating it by the spoonful for breakfast.

Whatever preserve you choose to provide for the future will bear traces of the past. The preserving arts, after all, are as old as the seasons of nature and the cunning of man in his need to evoke in the depths of winter the illusion of summer sun.

Homemade Tomato Ketchup

5 pounds ripe tomatoes
1 cup chopped onions
1 teaspoon each salt, mace, dry mustard,
   and cinnamon
½ teaspoon each ground cloves and
   black pepper
pinch cayenne pepper
1-2 tablespoons brown sugar
¼ cup red wine vinegar

Quarter tomatoes and remove cores. Stew with chopped onions in a covered enamel, stainless steel, or anodized aluminum pot for about 30 minutes. To make a smooth puree, put mixture, 2 cups at a time, in a blender or food mill. The blender will pulverize skins and seeds, while a food mill will make a uniform puree and will sieve out the skins and seeds. Mix the dry seasonings together (except for the sugar) and add to the puree. Return the puree to the pot and boil down until extremely thick, 30 minutes or more. Add 1 tablespoon of the sugar and taste before adding more, since the acidity of the tomatoes will vary. Add the vinegar and taste again. Adjust the sweetness and sourness to your taste. Ladle puree into sterilized jars or freezer containers.

Yields 3½–4 cups.

Double-Red Tomato Sauce

1 large sweet red bell pepper
2 pounds ripe tomatoes
½ cup chopped onion
1 clove garlic, minced
2 tablespoons olive oil
1 tablespoon butter
¼ teaspoon thyme
2 basil leaves
2 anchovy fillets, chopped
pinch black pepper

Roast the pepper under a broiler for 5–10 minutes, turning the pepper to blacken its skin on all sides. Put in a paper bag for 5 minutes to loosen skin before peeling it. Then remove stem and seeds. Loosen tomato skins by

immersing tomatoes for 1-2 minutes in boiling water. Remove skins, cores, and seeds. Put chopped onion and garlic in a saucepan with oil and butter and cook 5 minutes, or until soft. Add tomatoes and cook, covered, about 10 minutes.

Chop the red pepper and add to the tomatoes with all the seasonings. Cook, uncovered, about 5 minutes to blend flavors. Put in a food processor or through a food mill to make a fairly chunky puree. Don't overprocess.

Yields 3 cups.

Green Tomato Marmalade

2 pounds green tomatoes, chopped
1 orange, sliced thin
1 lemon, sliced thin
1-1½ cups sugar
3-4 tablespoons good wine vinegar
2 tablespoons fresh ginger root, finely chopped
½ teaspoon each salt and ground cloves
pinch cayenne pepper

If tomatoes are large, chop coarsely. If tomatoes are small (like cherry tomatoes), cut in half. Slice orange and lemon and remove seeds. Put in a wide-mouthed shallow pot for boiling together with sugar, vinegar, and seasonings. Use more or less sugar and vinegar according to the tartness of the tomatoes. Cover pot with lid for the first 5 minutes to release juices, then boil, uncovered, 20-30 minutes, or until liquid is thick and syrupy. Stir frequently to keep mixture from scorching. Mixture will thicken as it cools.

Yields 2 cups.

THE WELL–BRED RABBIT

Some countries are more countrified than others. When I think of country inns, I think of France, where I was awakened one morning by a gentle rhythmic thud, as if someone were playing softball. I peered into the court-yard below my window and saw the chef-patron in his apron bopping a row of rabbits with a bat, one hit each, in preparation for our noon meal. In France the scene was as natural and pastoral as the dawn.

I've since wondered why Americans have dropped rabbits from their daily menus. Was it the Depression that gave rabbits a bad name as a poor man's chicken? Or did the Easter and other bunnies and rabbits—Bugs, Peter, Br'er—become so human in our imaginations that we wanted to pet them, laugh at them, feed them, do anything but eat them? As a child, hearing the stories of Peter and Br'er, I was terrified equally of Farmer MacGregor and the Tar Baby, but that didn't prevent my forking into a tender rabbit thigh any more than the story of poor Chicken Little prevented my nibbling a crisp chicken breast. And I'm certain that I didn't sob when I was rocked to sleep with "Bye Bye Baby Bunting, Daddy's Gone A-Hunting."

Maybe Americans just got too urban for rabbits when we opted for factory chickens to replace our once infinite variety of   wild fowl and game. Now that commer-cial chicken has gone the way of all factory flesh, rabbit is surely due for a comeback. Rabbit flesh is firmer, leaner, and whiter than chicken and is as tasty as veal. If you live in the country, keep a garden, and are a good shot, you will have no trouble securing a constant supply of rabbits. If you live in the city, however, your rabbit may come frozen from Australia or Canada. Because their flesh is firmer, rabbits freeze better than chickens do, so the frozen form is not to be sneered at; but get fresh ones when you can.

In any European country, you can get your rabbits fresh at the butcher shop, hanging in rows by their feet, their long bodies neatly skinned with the heads left on to supply flavor for the sauce, perhaps a bit of fur left on the muzzle around the bunny incisors. Liver, heart, and lungs are left intact inside the chest cavity, and on each side of the backbone is a delicious kidney wrapped in its protective fat. It's the pair of kidneys that make a saddle of hare a royal dish.

To cut up a whole rabbit, you sever the head from the neck, then cut the body in four or six pieces. First cut the body in half below the ribs, then cut along the backbone to divide the two front legs. You can now divide the back and thighs into two large pieces or remove the thighs from the back and cut the back in two.

Every country, including our own, once valued for their size and gamy taste the large wild rabbits we call hares. Germans still marinate in wine and vinegar their sweet-sour *hasenpfeffers*, and the French still thicken with blood their rich *civets de lièvre*. We must look to the Italians, however, for simple country traditions in rabbit cookery, both domesticated and wild. Elizabeth David, in her 1954 *Italian Food*, in numbering the variety of birds that appear on Italian tables, remarks that "almost anything which flies—is killed and eaten in Italy." Change that to "almost anything which runs."

A recent foray into Umbria brought   me rabbit

in a dozen delectable ways. In medieval Gubbio—where St. Francis so lovingly chided a wolf for eating the good citizens that the wolf wept for shame and mended his ways (doubtless substituting rabbits for people)—I sat at La Taverna del Lupo and ate rabbit stuffed with fennel and roasted like pork. Elsewhere I feasted on rabbit flavored with juniper, with rosemary and sage, with garlic and lemon, with white wine and red. Elizabeth David mentions rabbit with marsala, with pine nuts and raisins, and other combinations that typify the early influence of the Middle East on the Veneto region.

One region that has maintained centuries-old traditions of rabbit cookery is the Southwest. In New Mexico I have tasted rabbit spiced with red chili and smoothed with ground nuts and seeds. South of the border, Latin Americans cook rabbit in dozens of ways. Elisabeth Lambert Ortiz, in her 1979 *Book of Latin American Cooking*, describes a favorite dish of the coastal region of Colombia, which stews a well-seasoned rabbit in coconut milk.

As the Indians of the New World have always done, so also can we thank our brother rabbit for the gift of himself to our table. His is one species, at least, that we cannot endanger—because wild or tame, in city or in country, the rabbit is a creature of infinite breeding.

Venetian Rabbit

One 3–4-pound rabbit (or hare, if you can get one),
   cut in pieces
salt and pepper to taste
½ cup flour, for dredging
2 tablespoons each butter and olive oil
¼ cup diced Italian ham
1 onion, diced

1 cup red wine
¼ cup each pine nuts and sultana raisins
rind of 1 lemon, grated
½ teaspoon ground cinnamon
¼ teaspoon ground cloves
1 teaspoon sugar

Season the rabbit pieces, dredge them in flour, salt, and pepper, and sauté them in hot butter and oil with the ham and onion. When the pieces are well browned, add the wine and remaining ingredients. Cover the pan tightly and simmer gently 1-1½ hours, or until tender.

Serves 4-6.

Grilled Rabbit with Fennel

1 whole rabbit, with liver, heart, and kidneys
salt and pepper to taste
½ cup fresh bread crumbs
1 small onion, chopped fine
2 cloves garlic, minced
1 cup chopped fennel tops
⅓ cup olive oil
1 tablespoon Pernod

Remove innards and season rabbit inside and out with salt and pepper. Chop the innards, mix them with the bread crumbs, onion, garlic, and fennel, and sauté quickly in 2 tablespoons of the olive oil. Add the Pernod for liquid. Stuff the cavity of the rabbit with the mixture and sew the flesh together with kitchen thread. Rub oil on the rabbit and place it on a grill or under a broiler.

Turn the rabbit so that it is seared   well on both sides. Cover the grill with a hood or   aluminum foil and lower the coals so that the rabbit can cook more slowly for about 30–45 minutes. If using a broiler, first sear the rabbit on both sides, then put it in a baking pan, cover it with foil, and bake it at 375° until tender. Either way, baste the rabbit with oil to keep it from drying out.

Serves 4–6.

Rabbit in Coconut Milk

One 3–4-pound rabbit, cut in pieces
2 tablespoons each butter and oil
1 large onion, chopped
3 cloves garlic, minced
2 roasted sweet red bell peppers, skinned
    and chopped
1 small hot red pepper, seeded and minced
1 large tomato, peeled, seeded, and chopped
1/2 teaspoon ground cumin
salt and pepper to taste
2 cups boiling chicken broth
1/2 cup coconut milk*

Sauté rabbit in the butter and oil until browned on all sides. Remove rabbit to a casserole. Sauté onion, garlic, and peppers for 2–3 minutes and add them to the rabbit. Sprinkle the rabbit with the chopped tomato and seasonings. Add the broth, bring to a simmer, cover tightly, and simmer very gently for about 1 1/2 hours, or until rabbit is

---

*In specialty and health food stores, we can get unsweetened grated coconut, which is often frozen. From grated coconut, fresh or frozen, you can make coconut milk by adding 2 cups of boiling water to a cup of grated coconut   in a blender. Blend well, then pour the liquid through   a strainer, pressing the coconut with a heavy spoon or   a pestle to extract the juice. To start with a whole

tender. Remove rabbit to a serving dish. Reduce liquid in the casserole by half. Over low heat, stir in the coconut milk and cook a very few minutes to thicken the sauce. Pour sauce over the rabbit.

Serves 4–6.

Rabbit in Lemon, Garlic, and Thyme

One 3-4-pound rabbit, cut in pieces
4 lemons
1/3 cup olive oil
1 onion, sliced
3 stalks celery, cut in sticks
salt and pepper to taste
8 cloves garlic
1½ teaspoons thyme
1 cup white wine

Marinate the rabbit pieces overnight in the juice of 2 of the lemons. Cut the other 2 lemons in slices. Sauté the onion and celery lightly in the olive oil and remove them to a plate. Pat the rabbit pieces dry, salt and pepper them, and sauté them quickly in the oil. Peel and mash the garlic cloves and add them to the oil with the onion, celery, thyme, lemon slices, and the lemon juice. Add the wine, bring to a simmer, cover tightly, and simmer slowly 45–60 minutes, or until the rabbit is tender.

Serves 4–6.

---

coconut, pierce two of the "eyes" with an ice pick and hammer, shake out and reserve the liquid inside, then heat the coconut at 400° for 15 minutes. Put a towel over the coconut and smash the shell with a hammer. Remove the hard shell from the pieces and put the coconut meat, brown skin and all, in a blender or food processor. Grate finely before adding boiling water.

THE PLEASURES
OF PLUMMING

"Within this Indian Orchard fruites be some, / The ruddie cherrie and the jettie Plumme," wrote William Wood in Massachusetts in 1635, describing the orchards that produced the plums for our first Thanksgiving dinner. Colonists discovered many kinds and colors of wild and cultivated plums, including the uniquely American beach plum. Long Island Indians so valued their beach plums that when they sold their lands to colonists they reserved "all liberty and privileges of plumming."

Today we have several hundred varieties of plums—in colors red, purple, blue, black, gold, and green—and a profusion of plum names such as damson, Santa Clara, Italian prune, angelino, royal, and greengage (which the French call *reine claude*). Some have extremely tart skins, while others, such as greengage, possess a juicy sweetness all the way through. Unripe plums of any kind are astringently tart, so let the buyer beware and let him also experiment in his plumming pleasures.

Nothing beats the taste of ripe plums in season, their taut skins bursting with juice. When I buy too many plums to eat raw, I bake them with something sweet like jelly and tart like orange. I might also put them in a nutty pastry crust or, on an Indian summer day, puree them to make a beautifully green or pink ice cream topped with a sprig of garden mint.

The Chinese have known for centuries the pleasures of combining the tart sweetness of plum puree with pork, duck, or chicken. Karen Lee, in her 1981 *Chinese Cooking for the American Kitchen,* incorporates Chinese plum sauce into a barbecue sauce for spareribs, which is equally delicious with grilled lamb. If you have a superfluity of overripe plums, you can make your own Chinese plum sauce by simmering pureed plums with chili peppers, ginger root, and Chinese five-spice powder (cinnamon, fennel, star anise, cloves, and Szechuan pepper).

In summer and fall, our American colonists went a-plumming to garner fruits for winter, fruits they could preserve by bottling, jellying, or drying. Amelia Simmons, in *American Cookery* (1796), advises putting damsons in empty stoppered snuff bottles before treating them to a boiling-water bath. She also suggests preserving unripe plums by "coddling" (simmering) them "till they are as green as grass."

Drying plums to make prunes was ancient knowledge for the colonists, but they handed down to us terms of a certain laxity. "Plum" once meant any kind of dried fruit, in addition to fresh plums, so that we still make English "plum" puddings and cakes that are stuffed with raisins and currants but nary a fresh plum nor dried prune.

Although all our plum varieties are members of the genus *Prunus,* today the word "prune" is not held in high repute. Because my family was addicted to prunes for reasons of internal plumbing, I thought I could never with pleasure look a prune in the face. That was before I discovered the joys of plumping prunes in brandy and eating them as a counter to fresh grapefruit or as a sauce for vanilla ice cream.

For plums dried or fresh, the Indians knew what they were about in preserving their privileges of plumming.

Plum-Barbecued Ribs

2 racks lean spareribs (4 pounds)
1 cup red plum puree
8 slices fresh ginger root
3 green onions, chopped
2 to 3 cloves garlic, mashed
3 tablespoons sherry
2 tablespoons dark soy sauce
1 tablespoon tomato puree
1/2 teaspoon mixed cinnamon and cloves
dash of Tabasco or cayenne pepper
1/2 cup honey

Trim excess fat from ribs and make a shallow cut with a knife between each. Combine remaining ingredients, except for the honey, and marinate ribs in the mixture in the refrigerator for 6–8 hours. Just before grilling or roasting, dribble honey over the ribs. For oven roasting, roast the ribs for 50 minutes, first fat side up, then turning them over halfway through and basting them with the marinade. Turn the heat up to 450° for a final 10 minutes' browning, fat side up. Cut ribs into hunks and serve.

Serves 4.

Orange-Glazed Plums

1 pound plums (ripe but firm)
1/2–1 cup currant jelly
rind and juice of 1 orange

Place whole plums in a single layer in a buttered baking dish. Melt the jelly and pour it over the plums. Grate orange rind, squeeze juice, and add to the plums. Cover the baking dish and bake at 250° for 30–45 minutes, depending on type, size, and ripeness of plums. For a thicker syrup remove plums carefully and boil down the juice. Pour over the plums and serve hot or cold.

Serves 4.

Walnut-Plum Tart

3/4 cup walnuts
3/4 cup sugar
3/4 cup flour
1/4 pound (1 stick) butter, melted
1 recipe Orange-Glazed Plums, baked as above

Grind the walnuts in a processor with the sugar. Mix with the flour and butter and press mixture onto the bottom and sides of a 9-inch pie pan. Bake at 350° for 15–20 minutes, watching to see that the nuts don't burn. Remove pits from the baked plums and place plums, cut side down, in the crust. Glaze with a little thickened syrup.

Serves 4–6.

Fresh Plum Ice Cream

1 pound sweet-skinned plums,
    such as greengage (for 2 cups puree)
½ cup superfine sugar, or to taste
2–3 tablespoons lemon juice
2 cups heavy cream
¼ teaspoon almond extract

Halve plums and remove the pits.

Puree the fruit in a processor or food mill. Stir in the remaining ingredients and taste for sweetness and sourness, adding more sugar or lemon as desired. Pour mixture into the container of an electric or hand-cranked freezer, or freeze it in a metal tray in the refrigerator. Re-whip the ice cream mixture in a processor just before serving.

Yields about 1 quart.

October

October

MUSHROOMS WILD AND TAME

Mushroom Ketchup

Finger-Food Oyster Mushrooms

Shiitake Mushroom Soup

Wild Mushroom Sauté

Chanterelles Quail

ON THE SUBJECT OF PORK

A Mild Wet Cure for Pork

Grilled Pork Loin with Herbs

Braised Pork with Leeks and Sweet Potato

Baked Pork and Apple Pie

APPLE TIME

Normandy Apple-Nut Salad

Roast Chicken with Apples and Fennel

Sugarless Apple-Pear Butter

Taffety Tart

Apple Tansy

MUSHROOMS
WILD AND TAME

Once upon a time all mushrooms were wild, but in America they stayed wild until this century. Even in urban Philadelphia, Eliza Leslie, in her 1837 *Directions for Cooking*, advises the maker of "Mushroom Catchup" to "Take mushrooms that have been freshly gathered, and examine them carefully to ascertain that they are of the right sort." Perhaps too many careless examiners caused Americans to declare *Agaricus bisporus* the *only* right sort. Pennsylvanians in the early 1900s began to cultivate this type in limestone caves in Chester County, and today *A. bisporus* is the white supermarket mushroom that we now eat 550 million pounds of each year.

In Europe the French had cultivated this species from the time of Louis XIV. The little white buttons called *champignons de Paris* appeared on Edwardian tables *sous cloche*, or under glass bell jars. In the Orient the Japanese had been cultivating shiitake and matsukame mushrooms since the second century A.D. One man's "wild" mushroom is another man's "tame." The advantage of tamed varieties is that they are available without regard to season, weather, or woodland. The disadvantage is that they narrow the mushroom palate to but a handful of the 40,000 edible species available to those who know mushroom right from wrong.

Ironically, we Americans are only now rediscovering our native wildings, often by way of similar types of mushrooms imported expensively from abroad. Of course our local mycologists have scoured their neighboring woods for years, tracking down morels in the spring, tree oysters in summer, chanterelles in fall. But now untutored mushroom lovers can benefit from the mushroom explosion that brought us in 1986 *Joe's Book of Mushroom Cookery*, in which Jack Czarnecki, of Joe's Restaurant in Reading, Pennsylvania, has condensed the lore of three generations of mushroom hunter-cooks. Jack of *Joe's* tells us how to dry, pickle, freeze, blanch, extract, puree, braise, and stir-fry each mushroom kind according to its unique character—the smoky shiitake, the nutty morel, the briny tree oyster, the earthy cepe or porcini, the apricot-scented chanterelle.

I've space for only a brief sampling of our rich mushroom world, beginning with an updated version of Miss Leslie's "Mushroom Catchup." Her ketchup we would call a soy, since she salts fresh mushrooms in layers, sets them by the fire for twenty-four hours to draw out their juice, then squeezes the juice through a bag to make a spicy mushroom extract. Of course you can buy mushroom-flavored soy sauce in Chinese grocery stores, but Miss Leslie's sauce is more like a mushroom extract, with which you can enrich a soup, a sauce, a fish fillet, a hamburger, a chicken breast, an omelet, a stir-fry.

To make use of whole mushrooms, I've deep-fried the tree oyster or oyster mushroom because its firm texture makes it a good finger food. For a soup I've chosen the shiitake for its rich flavor and meaty texture; the stems enrich the broth, while the sliced caps make a meal. If you prefer a thicker soup, add some mushroom ketchup.

A mushroom sauté can include a mixture of whatever wild and tame mushrooms you want to sample for a comparison of taste and texture. Reconstituted dried mushrooms will bind and intensify these tastes in a sauce, and cream will enrich and smooth them. The affinity of mushrooms and cream we learn from a recipe in Martha Washington's *Booke of Cookery* (1749). If you wish "To Dress a Dish of Mushrumps," you are to stew them with onion, parsley, nutmeg, fresh butter, and sweet, thick cream.

As a garnish for game, I've picked the orange chanterelle, following Jack Czarnecki's suggestion that dried apricots intensify the peppery apricot flavor of this beauty and that the combination does wonders with quail.

The abundance of mushroom varieties now in our markets should send us scurrying into the fall woods with our baskets and an expert in tow to help us examine carefully the wild mushrooms that we will tame in our cooking pots, provided of course that they are of "the right sort."

Mushroom Ketchup

½ pound domestic mushrooms, chopped
4 green onions, sliced thin
1 small clove garlic, minced
2 tablespoons butter
1 teaspoon each sea salt and black pepper
¼ teaspoon each sugar, cloves, mace,
   and allspice
1 teaspoon each soy sauce and brandy

Sauté mushrooms, onions, and garlic in the butter 2-3 minutes. Add salt, pepper, and powdered seasonings and sauté 2-3 minutes more. Turn mixture into a blender. Add soy and brandy and puree until smooth. Keeps well refrigerated.

Yields about ⅔ cup.

Finger-Food Oyster Mushrooms

½ pound whole oyster mushrooms
salt and pepper
1 cup flour, for dredging
1 egg, beaten
⅓ cup heavy cream
2 cups fresh bread crumbs
oil for deep frying

Sprinkle mushrooms with salt and pepper and roll them in the flour. Beat egg with the cream. Dip each mushroom in the egg and cream mixture and then roll each in the bread crumbs. Heat oil 2 inches deep in a frying pan until hot but not smoking (375°) and fry the mushrooms 2 or 3 at a time. Remove them with a slotted spoon and drain on paper towels. Sprinkle with salt if desired.

Serves 4.

Shiitake Mushroom Soup

½ pound fresh shiitake mushrooms
6 cups beef stock
2 tablespoons butter
4 green onions, slivered
½ clove garlic, minced
4 slices fresh ginger root, minced
1 teaspoon soy sauce
½ teaspoon each salt and sugar
¼ teaspoon black pepper, or to taste
2 tablespoons chopped coriander

Separate caps of mushrooms from stems. Chop stems and add them to the beef stock. Bring stock to a boil, cover, simmer 20 minutes, strain stock, and discard stems. Slice mushroom caps and sauté them in the butter over high heat with the onions, garlic, and ginger root. Add them to the beef stock, taste for seasoning, and add soy, salt, sugar, and pepper with care, depending on the taste of the stock. Garnish soup bowls with the coriander.

Serves 4.

Wild Mushroom Sauté

½ ounce dried mushrooms, cepe or porcini
1 cup hot chicken stock
6 large wild mushrooms
6 domestic mushrooms
4 tablespoons butter
3 green onions, minced
1 clove garlic, minced
salt and pepper to taste
2 tablespoons red wine
¼ cup heavy cream
¼ cup fresh chopped tarragon

Soak the dried mushrooms in hot stock for 20 minutes. Remove mushrooms, rinse them if they are sandy, and slice them if the pieces are large. Strain the stock through a double layer of paper towels lining a sieve and set aside. Slice the fresh mushrooms ¼-inch thick. Heat half the butter in a large frying pan. Sauté the dried mushrooms first, then add the fresh mushrooms with the onions, garlic, salt, and pepper. Sauté over high heat until browned. Add the wine and stock and bring to a boil. Add remaining butter and heavy cream, whipped until frothy. Sprinkle with tarragon and serve.

Serves 4.

Chanterelles Quail

¾ pound fresh chanterelle mushrooms
1 small onion, minced
¼ pound (1 stick) butter
¼ cup finely chopped dried apricots
4 slices white bread, crusts removed
4 quail
salt and pepper to taste
2 tablespoons olive oil
2 tablespoons Madeira

Slice the mushrooms with their stems. Mince 1 cup of these sliced mushrooms. Sauté the onion in half the butter (4 tablespoons) for 3–4 minutes. Add the minced mushrooms and chopped apricots and sauté 3 or 4 minutes more. Set aside. Melt 2 tablespoons of the remaining butter and brush the bread with it. Put bread on a baking sheet and bake at 350° for 10 minutes, or until toasted. Spread the mushroom mixture on the toast and place on serving plates.

Butterfly the quail by cutting each bird open along the backbone and pressing it flat. Sprinkle both sides with salt and pepper. Heat remaining butter and the oil in a large skillet and sauté the quail over high heat until browned on both sides, about 5 minutes per side. Place the quail on the toast. Sauté the remaining sliced mushrooms over high heat (add more oil and butter if needed) for 2–3 minutes. Add the Madeira, scrape juices from the pan, and pour mushrooms and juice over the quail.

Serves 4.

ON THE SUBJECT
OF PORK

"Look at Pork. There's a subject!" Dickens wrote in *Great Expectations*. "If you want a subject, look at Pork!" In Dickens's day, most Americans who looked at pork found it a worthy subject at any time of year, but especially in the fall. After the farmer had dug his parsnips for the root cellar and buried his cabbages in the ground, it was time to butcher his hog, render its lard, and carve its flesh into joints, bacons, and hams. These he would store down-cellar in a pork barrel covered with a stone to keep it safe from rats, flies, and politicians.

Pork was almost never eaten "fresh," that is, untreated. Any part of the leg, shoulder, or loin, whether for roasting or boiling, was usually given a brief "salt cure." Pork that was kept in the barrel for weeks or months was called "pickled pork," some parts of which were smoked after pickling to make bacons and hams. As any smoker today knows, smoked meat in order to last must first be cured with salt, because meat decays faster than smoking can dry and preserve it. If our American farmer came from France, he called his cured meat *petit salé;* if from England, he called it "corned," since the English use the word "corn" to refer to any grains, including grains of salt.

If we look at the subject of pork, we learn that "to cure" means "to care for," "to treat," or "to restore to health." When applied to food, curing means maintaining or restoring the health or goodness of a food by treating it with care. Lydia Child, in *The American Frugal Housewife* (1829), spoke for centuries of farm wisdom when she said, "The slight sickness occasioned by eating roasted pork may be prevented by soaking it in salt and water the night before you cook it." Because curing was important for flavor as well as health, the *Genesee Farmer* (1831) could report, "Perhaps there is no subject of equal interest among farmers, on which there is such a contrariety of opinion, as that of curing hams."

Every farmer claimed that the superior flavor and wholesomeness of his own pork was owing to his recipe for a cure, whether he used Liverpool salt for a dry cure or rain or well water for a wet cure. One *Genesee Farmer* contributor outlined "the whole secret of making good pickled pork for family use": as soon as the hog is dressed, pack the pieces in a barrel with plenty of salt on all sides, roll the barrel to the pump and fill it with water, lay on a flat stone to keep the pork under the pickle, and finally put the barrel in the cellar, "covered so as to exclude the flies, and there it remains until a piece is wanted."

Neither flies nor politicians, but ice, changed the nature of the pork barrel by the mid-nineteenth century. With refrigeration, bacon and ham required far less salt in the curing, and shoulders and loins required no cure at all. Jane Grigson, in her *British Cookery* (1985), notes that American ice transformed English bacon when a butcher named Harris visited America in 1847 and returned home to build England's first commercial ice-house in 1856. In our enthusiasm for technology, Americans threw out the pork barrel and brought in the icebox, abandoning curing of any kind, except for bacon and ham. One result is a loss of flavor in today's pork dishes.

Even when we don't need to preserve pork, we might look at old ways of curing pork to restore

that lost flavor. Proportions and seasonings vary widely, but for flavor we don't need a pound of salt for every 10 pounds of meat, which was once the standard proportion for preserving. Sugar is now a standard addition because sugar helps to tenderize the meat as the salt draws its juices from it. Other seasonings, such as peppercorns, juniper, bay leaves, allspice or cloves, rosemary, and thyme, vary according to the taste of the pickler.

Here I've used a wet cure, or brine, rather than a dry cure because brine works faster in imparting flavor to the meat. A mild wet cure will work its magic in twelve to forty-eight hours. For stronger flavor, you can leave the meat in the brine (under refrigeration) for as long as two weeks before cooking. You can then cook the pork just as you would uncured meat, only the cooking time will be shorter because the meat will be more tender.

Because curing speeds cooking time, even an overnight cure is good for a boned loin that might be roasted or grilled. For flavor and speed, the Chinese often use a soy and sherry marinade to cure what they call "red-cooked pork," the red color resulting from the soy soak. Here I've used a simple Anglo-French brine to tenderize a loin that will grill quickly over hot coals to form the centerpiece for grilled garden vegetables.

Boiling was the traditional cooking method for pickled pork, but "braising" is a more accurate term for the simmering of a pork leg or shoulder in white wine, flavored with strips of leek and sweet potatoes, to make a beautiful one-dish meal as good cold as hot. If wine seems too Frenchified, look at *Mrs. Putnam's Receipt Book* (1858), wherein she suggests adding to her pork "a bottle of champagne, or a pint of good white wine vinegar." In her *New Receipts for Cooking* (1852), Eliza Leslie suggests balancing cider vinegar with brown sugar and further sweetening the liquid with chestnuts or sweet potatoes.

When vinegar was added to the cooking liquid of pork, cured pork was often said to be "soused."

The scrappier pieces of a cured leg, shoulder, or loin can be finely chopped and turned into a traditional English pork and apple pie, like one of the standing pork pies made famous by the town of Melton Mowbray and favored still by New England cooks. Many recipes advise moistening the contents of this deep-dish pie with wine or ale, but I find that the pork, apples, and onions alone are so sweet and moist that I simply add a grated raw potato to soak up extra liquid.

On a recent trip to Louisiana, where some country traditions are as strong as they were in Dickens's day, I found a black taxi driver who considered the subject of pork. He told me that when he was a kid they'd go to the store and look in the pork barrel and buy a piece only if it was nice and lean. But now, he says, he can't find pickled pork at all, and even fresh pork doesn't taste the same as in his mama's mama's day. Maybe the cure for today's fresh pork is to cure it.

A Mild Wet Cure for Pork

One 6-pound piece of pork (leg, shoulder, loin, etc.)
3-4 quarts water (or to cover)
½ cup kosher or sea salt
½ cup sugar
1 teaspoon each peppercorns and juniper berries, crushed
2 bay leaves, crushed
1 clove garlic, mashed
3-4 allspice berries, crushed
3 sprigs each fresh rosemary and thyme

Trim the meat of excess fat and bone it or not, as you wish. Bring the water to a boil with all the seasonings and let it cool. Put the pork in a crock or glass bowl, cover it with the brine, and weight the meat with a heavy jar or plate to make sure the brine entirely covers the meat. Refrigerate for 12-48 hours, or longer if you like, before braising, roasting, or grilling.

Grilled Pork Loin with Herbs

One 4-6-pound boned and cured pork loin
⅓ cup olive oil
1 tablespoon black peppercorns, crushed
3 tablespoons fresh thyme, minced
1 cup hot meat stock
Garnish: any or all of the following vegetables—
grilled red peppers, eggplant strips, halved onions, whole garlic heads

Drain meat and pat it dry. Roll and tie it with stout string. Rub it well with the oil. Mix the pepper and thyme and sprinkle all over the meat. Grill the pork 25-35 minutes, turning it constantly to sear the fat evenly. Cook to an interior temperature of 150° to 160°. Put the roast on a hot serving platter, pour the hot meat stock over it, and let it sit 10 minutes before slicing. Surround with the grilled vegetables. Good at room temperature.
Serves 8-12.

Braised Pork with Leeks and Sweet Potato

One 6-pound piece of cured pork
2 large carrots
2 stalks celery
2 large leeks
1 sweet potato
3 cups white wine
1 cup brine (or meat stock)
2 sprigs rosemary or thyme

Drain the pork from the brine, reserve the brine, and put the pork in a pot with the fat side up. Bake at 325° for about an hour to brown the fat. Remove and pour off all the melted fat. Slice the carrots and celery crosswise; slice the leeks and potato lengthwise, in strips about ½ inch wide and 4 inches long. Put the wine and reserved brine or stock into a pot large enough to hold the meat and vegetables. Bring the liquid to a boil, add the leeks, and cook 5 minutes. Add the meat and remaining vegetables and herbs, and more wine or stock if necessary to cover the meat. Bring to a simmer, cover, and bake 30–60 minutes at 300° (liquid should barely simmer), or until a meat thermometer registers 150° to 160°.

Serves 8–12.

Baked Pork and Apple Pie

1 large onion, minced
4 tablespoons butter
2 tart apples
2 tablespoons minced parsley
1 teaspoon chopped fresh sage
   (½ teaspoon dried)
½ teaspoon salt
¼ teaspoon each dried thyme and black pepper
1 medium potato
4 cups cured pork cut in small cubes
pie crust or biscuit dough for a 9-inch deep-dish
   pie top

Soften the minced onion 3-4 minutes in butter in a sauté pan. Core, quarter, and pare the apples and slice them. Mix the seasonings and then grate the potato (so that once it's grated you can proceed to the next step before it turns brown). In a deep baking dish, put half the pork, cover it with half the onion, potato, apples, and seasonings; and repeat. Cover the top of the dish with the crust or biscuit dough and bake at 400° for 25-40 minutes, or until the crust is well browned.

Serves 4-6.

APPLE TIME

In October, brightness falls from the air in a shower of red, green, and gold globes, bearing names as resonant as Orleans Reinette, as exotic as Mutsu, as down-home as Sheepnose. Put them all together, all 6,000 named varieties of them, and they spell A-P-P-L-E. Ever since Adam, the apple has redeemed the fall.

Ever since Eve caused the fall—and other seasons—by eating an apple raw, apples have been the mainstay of winter fruits because of their keeping ability and cooking powers. Apples can be juiced to cider, reduced to "butter," concentrated to jelly, pureed to sauce, distilled into brandy, dried in spirals, or packed whole and kept fresh in barrels of wood chips or sand for midwinter omelets, puddings, fritters, salads, and pies.

Our New England forebears survived many an icy winter on apples grown from seeds they brought across the Atlantic in their pockets, along with recipes dating back to the invasion of Britain by Rome. "Have made 90 Barrels of Cyder," a Boston housewife wrote in the 1750s, "and at same time consumed 100 Bushils of Apples in the Family. The Children almost Live upon 'em when ripe."

A lot of those bushels went into tarts and pies, as they had done for so many centuries in England that colonists may well have said "as English as apple pie." In Chaucer's time, a standing crust was often filled with apples and meat or meat fat, as in mincemeat, for a main dish. For a sweetmeat, apples were combined with candied orange and lemon peel to fill a pastry shell. Elizabethan poets were wont to compare the sweet breath of their ladies to "the steame of apple pyes." Such steam was sweetened by rose water or orange water in the "taffety tarts" popular in the seventeenth and eighteenth centuries, and were often further perfumed with fennel or anise. What was called "tartstuff" in the same period meant apple puree spiked with aromatics like cinnamon and ginger and strong waters like claret.

Here I've made a taffety tart by combining candied citrus (here a bitter orange marmalade) with a tartstuff of sugarless apple and pear puree, made in the time-honored way of reducing apple cider to "butter." In her *Domestic Cookery* of 1845, a Quaker housewife of English lineage, Elizabeth Ellicott Lea, advises that the best way to make apple butter is to boil cider fresh from the press in a large copper kettle. When it is reduced by half, add apples and quince or pears, and stir with "a stick made of hickory wood, somewhat like a common hoe, with holes in it." Reduced to a thick silken pulp, the fruit needs no sweetness other than its own. Thinned with heavy cream, the puree makes an extraordinary caramel-colored sauce for fresh fruit salad, fruit soufflé, or ice cream.

From England comes a dessert omelet of apples and eggs called "tansy." Originally the omelet was flavored with a green herb such as tansy leaves, but it came to mean any apple-filled omelet, such as the one in Martha Washington's *Booke of Cookery.* A nice way "To Make an Apple Tansie," Martha advises, is to shred apples into eggs beaten with rose water and cream and sprinkled with lemon peel. I've substituted calvados or rum for the rose water, but you could also use vanilla or almond flavoring.

The Norman conquest added to Anglo-Saxon traditions the French use of apples in dishes heartier than sweets. We can trace America's own Waldorf salad back

to the Caux region of Normandy, which still makes a potato salad with apples and nuts in a cream dressing. The Normans have also bequeathed to us their love of roasted pork, duck, or chicken flavored with apples and cream. Here I've added fennel to the roast chicken to give a good medieval crunch to the softer apple. You could substitute anise seed or, for a change of pace, some freshly grated ginger root.

In apple time nobody needs a recipe to make a meal of an apple sliced into hot butter and browned with a sprinkling of sugar. In winter nobody needs to be told how to roast an apple in a foil pan by the fireside. Some things are as natural as sin. Despite Adam's cavils, we owe Eve a lot, for if she brought on winter, she also brought, by way of apples, our happy fall.

Normandy Apple-Nut Salad

2 cups cooked and diced new potatoes
½ cup chopped celery
¼ cup shredded prosciutto or
    Smithfield ham
2 cups apples, diced
¾ cup walnuts, chopped
⅓ cup walnut or olive oil
1-2 tablespoons good wine vinegar
2 tablespoons sour cream
salt and pepper to taste
1 tablespoon freshly grated horseradish (optional)

Mix first five ingredients. Mix the remaining ingredients for the dressing, toss with apple mixture, and serve on lettuce leaves.

Serves 4.

Roast Chicken with Apples and Fennel

3 tart apples
2 green onions, chopped
One 3–4-pound roasting chicken (with giblets)
salt and pepper to taste
4 tablespoons softened butter
½ head of fennel, cut lengthwise
¼ cup heavy cream
lemon juice (optional)

Core, quarter, pare, and dice one of the apples. Combine with chopped green onions and a minced chicken liver to make a stuffing. Season with salt and pepper and sauté the mixture lightly in 1 tablespoon of butter (1–2 minutes) before stuffing cavity of chicken. Truss chicken with one string around the legs and one around the wings. Spread chicken with remaining butter, season with salt and pepper, and roast breast side down at 450° for 15 minutes. Turn breast side up and roast another 15 minutes.

Meanwhile, core, quarter, and pare the other two apples and slice them lengthwise. Trim fennel of outer layers, cut head in half, and slice crosswise finely. Pile apple and fennel slices around and over the chicken, pour on cream, and cover with foil. Bake 20–30 minutes, or until juice from the thigh runs clear. Add a squeeze or two of lemon juice if the apples seem too sweet.

Serves 4.

Sugarless Apple-Pear Butter

1 gallon apple cider
6 pears (about 3 pounds)
4 tart apples (1½–2 pounds)

Boil cider in a wide-mouthed kettle until it is reduced by half. Chop pears and apples and add them—skin, seeds, and all—to the kettle. Boil until fruit is reduced to a thick pulp. Strain through a large sieve, pressing fruit through with a sturdy spoon. To smooth out the puree, liquefy it in a blender.
Yields about 2½ cups.

Taffety Tart

2 tart apples (Granny Smiths or greenings)
2 tablespoons butter
½ cup bitter orange marmalade
2 tablespoons lemon juice (or to taste)
1 cup apple-pear butter
1 9-inch prebaked pie shell

Core, quarter, and pare apples and cut in thick slices. Sauté slices in butter over a high flame until browned but still firm. Remove and set aside. Add marmalade and lemon juice to the pan and stir until marmalade melts. Cover pie shell with a layer of the apple-pear butter, add the sliced apples, and pour the marmalade mixture over the top.
Serves 6.

Apple Tansy

2 sweet apples (Mutsu or Golden Delicious)
2 eggs, separated
½ cup sugar
¼ cup flour
¼ teaspoon grated nutmeg
2 tablespoons calvados or rum
2 tablespoons butter
powdered sugar or grated lemon rind to garnish

Core, quarter, and pare the apples. Shred apples either in a processor or by hand. Beat egg yolks, sugar, flour, nutmeg, and calvados into the apples. Beat egg whites until stiff and fold into the apple mixture. Heat butter until bubbly in a nonstick skillet, add apple mixture, and sauté over medium heat until bottom of omelet is browned (2-3 minutes). Invert omelet onto a plate and slide back into skillet to brown the other side. Sprinkle with powdered sugar or grated lemon rind.

Serves 4.

November

OUR NATIVE NUTS

Southern Pecan Stuffing

Nut Pâté

Sea Trout with Pine Nuts and Coriander

Hickory Nut Cake

WILD BIRDS TAMED

Braised Turkey with Popcorn Stuffing

Braised Pheasant with Leeks

Quail Salad

FROSTY BEAUTIES:
PUMPKINS AND PERSIMMONS

Pumpkin Yeast Bread

Pumpkin and Lentil Salad

Persimmon Sweet-Potato Pone

Persimmon Fool

OUR NATIVE NUTS

Like many city folk removed to the country, I learned about our native black walnuts the hard way. After moving to an eighteenth-century farm in New Jersey, I was so delighted to find the woods thick with round, black pods that I picked a full bushel basket before I perceived that my brown-stained hands were going to stay brown— indefinitely. Had I known what the Lenape Indians knew, I would have used the husks, as they did, to dye my hair instead of my hands. I would also have known to dry the nuts before trying to open them, using a stone rather than a hammer to crack their obdurate shells. At any rate, I learned why black walnuts, despite their intense flavor, have not overtaken the more common English walnut.

More patient and more skillful, our Indian forebears knew how to use the abundant nuts of the wilderness— black walnuts, hickory, pecan, hazel, beech, butternut, chestnut, acorn, and piñon pine. Indians understood the nutritious qualities of nuts so well that they used them for protein and fat. They ground nuts with water to make nut "milk" the way we soak grated coconut today to make coconut milk. They also boiled finely ground nuts with fine cornmeal to make a pabulum for babies. Some nuts they mashed and boiled, then skimmed off the oil or "butter." Other nuts they ground to a paste, which they dried, ground again, and toasted to make a flour for stews, dumplings, ash cakes, and breads.

Edward Johnson in 1654 recounted in his *Wonder-Working Providence of Sions Saviour in New England* how the Narragansetts sweetened their Indian meal with wild chestnuts. "Boiled chestnuts," he explained, "is their white bread." Unfortunately, a fungus in the late nineteenth century wiped out the American chestnut, and today we must rely on the less sweet European or Chinese varieties.

The piñon pine, on the other hand, still flourishes in the Southwest, although the labor required to pick nuts from cones makes this Indian staple as costly as caviar. When Frank Hamilton Cushing collected recipes for *Zuni Breadstuff* in 1884, pine nuts were as common as corn. The Zunis heated the nuts in roasting trays, then rolled them on a lava stone to break their shells. They parched the kernels again and ground them fine in order to shape them into cylinders flavored with juniper berries or cedar sprigs; they then encased them in leaves and threw them into "the boiling basket" with heated stones. Sometimes they mixed the ground nuts with cornmeal to make griddle cakes on the hearth, or they made "stone-cakes," in which they alternated the nut batter with hot sandstone slabs, then cemented the layered stack with mud, burying the whole in a hot pit for baking.

In the recipes here I've used a variety of nuts in a variety of ways to show how rich is our nutted heritage. For a Thanksgiving turkey there is Blanche Rhett's Southern Pecan Stuffing in *200 Years of Charleston Cooking* (1930). Blanche had the recipe from Edward Hughes, who had it from his mother, who pronounced it "The most delicious stuffing that has ever been made."

To *The Kansas Home Cook-Book* (1874), published by The Kansas Home for the Friendless, a Mrs. T. L. Johnson contributed a friendly Hickory Nut Cake, leavened both by egg whites and the then new Peerless baking powder. This cake is also delicious made with black walnuts. To show how modern health and vegetarian movements recapitulate Indian uses of nuts, I've adapted a recipe for Nut Pâté from Anna Thomas's *The Vegetarian Epicure* (1972). Finally, to show how Indians used nuts as both a butter and a thickening, I've created a pine nut–garlic–coriander sauce, on the order of a pesto sauce, in which to bake a delicate fish.

In an ideal world we would not have to substitute filberts for hickory nuts, English walnuts for black ones, or imported chestnuts for native ones. But civilization brings its discontents, and what we have lost in flavor we have gained in ease. Nonetheless, we should not allow the black walnut and hickory nut to go the way of the great auk, and if any neighbor comes round in autumn with a basket of husked and shelled wild nut meats, I'll gladly cook up a storm.

Southern Pecan Stuffing

turkey giblets and broth or water to cover
¼ pound (1 stick) butter
1 large onion, chopped
¼ pound mushrooms, chopped
4 cups bread crumbs
2 tablespoons minced parsley
1 teaspoon each salt, pepper, celery seed, thyme, and nutmeg
¼ teaspoon ground mace
½ cup dry sherry
6 hard-cooked eggs, chopped fine
2 cups salted pecans, chopped

Simmer gizzard and heart in turkey broth and chop giblets fine. Melt half the butter in a large skillet, add the liver, and sauté it just enough to stiffen it. Chop the liver and add to the giblets. In the remaining butter, sauté the onion until soft, then add mushrooms and brown them 1-2 minutes. Add the bread crumbs, seasonings, and sherry and mix well. Fold in the eggs and nuts and taste for seasoning.

Yields about 8 cups stuffing, enough for a 12-pound turkey.

Nut Pâté

1 medium onion, chopped
2 cloves garlic, minced
3 tablespoons butter
2 cups cooked and peeled chestnuts, chopped
½ cup brandy
1 tablespoon Worcestershire sauce
¼ cup chopped parsley
¼ teaspoon each cumin, thyme, rosemary, paprika, and black pepper
½ teaspoon salt, or to taste
⅔ cup fresh bread crumbs
2 cups walnuts, chopped
¾ cup pecans, chopped
2 eggs, beaten
¼ cup grated Parmesan cheese

Sauté onions and garlic in the butter until soft. In a blender puree ½ cup of the chestnuts with the brandy and Worcestershire sauce. Add parsley and seasonings to the bread crumbs and sauté 3-4 minutes with the onions. Mix in the puree and remaining ingredients except for the cheese. Pack mixture into a standard loaf pan and sprinkle top with the grated cheese. Cover with foil and bake at 350° for 30 minutes. Remove foil and brown cheese, about 10 minutes. Serve hot or cold.

Serves 8-10.

Sea Trout with Pine Nuts and Coriander

1 cup pine nuts
1/3 cup olive oil
2 pounds sea trout or other fish fillets,
    such as brook trout, flounder, or cod
1/4 cup fresh lime juice
3-4 cloves garlic
1/4 cup coriander leaves
2 tablespoons parsley
1/2 teaspoon each salt and pure chili powder
black and cayenne peppers to taste

In a baking dish large enough to hold the fish in one layer, toast half the pine nuts in 2-3 tablespoons oil in a 350° oven for 5-8 minutes. Remove nuts and reserve for garnish. Place fish in the baking dish. Put remaining nuts and the rest of the ingredients in a blender and puree until sauce is only slightly chunky. Pour sauce over the fish and cover tightly with foil. Bake at 350° for 8-15 minutes (depending on thickness of fillets). Remove foil and sprinkle fish with reserved nuts.

Serves 4.

Hickory Nut Cake

¼ pound (1 stick) butter
2 cups powdered sugar
3½ cups cake flour
1 tablespoon baking powder
pinch salt
⅔ cup cold milk
1 teaspoon vanilla extract
¼ teaspoon almond extract
8 egg whites
2 cups hickory nuts or unskinned filberts,
  chopped

Cream butter with half the sugar. Mix flour with baking powder and salt. Mix milk with vanilla and almond extracts. Add flour and milk alternately to the butter. Beat egg whites until soft peaks form. Gradually beat in the remaining sugar. Fold egg whites into the batter and add the nuts. Spoon batter into a greased and floured Bundt pan or angel food cake pan. Bake at 375° for 30–40 minutes, or until a cake tester comes out clean. Cool in the pan 15 minutes before turning out onto a cake rack.

Serves 12.

WILD BIRDS TAMED

I like to think that one of the main topics of conversation between Chief Massasoit and Governor Bradford at their first Thanksgiving party in 1621 was how best to cook a turkey. England had been cooking turkeys for a good century before any Pilgrim set foot in Plymouth, thanks to Cortez and other conquistadors, who took the large dew-lapped birds, domesticated by the Aztecs, home to Spain. England liked to put these big birds into Christmas pies or display them as magnificent centerpieces in their full array of feathers, as they did peacocks and swans. Massasoit, on the other hand, probably preferred his turkeys roasted on a spit, especially if they were the thirty- to forty-pounders common in the wild of his time.

The problem with wild turkeys old enough to provide meat of that poundage was toughness. Governor Bradford, accustomed to boned turkey well spiced and baked in a quantity of butter in a thick pie crust, might have muttered some version of the rhyme,

> *Turkey boiled is turkey spoiled*
> *And turkey roast is turkey lost,*
> *But for turkey braised*
> *The Lord be praised.*

Braising wild turkey even today, when most weigh no more than six to twelve pounds, is the best way to guaran-

tee that the bird's flesh will be moist and tender instead
of dry and tough. Braising is also a good way to cook any
small domestic turkey under twelve pounds, because roasting is apt to dry out the white meat.

Even in the American wild, turkeys boiled, roasted,
or braised were also stuffed, because large birds served
as convenient pots for smaller birds and game, as well as
for porridges and pottages, vegetables and fruits. Fashionable stuffings for turkeys in the England our Pilgrims
left behind included bread crumbs mixed with minced
meat, herbs, dried fruit, crystallized oranges, and such
spices as cloves. Lacking these delicacies in the New
World, Pilgrim cooks would most likely have turned to
native grain, to turkey corn, to stuff their turkey cocks.
We know that Massasoit's brother, Quadequina, brought
popcorn to the first Thanksgiving and that the colonists
called it "parching corn" or "rice corn." Since Indians
were accustomed to grind popped corn as they did fresh
and dried corn, it's not unlikely that colonists sometimes
used ground popped corn instead of corn pone in their
stuffings.

At any rate, today's popcorn, ground in a processor
or food mill, makes an unusually delicious stuffing for
birds wild or tamed because it keeps its crunch, a bit like
wild rice or kasha, while absorbing flavors and juices. Try
it in a small braised turkey, capon, duck, or goose and
you'll discover that if the Pilgrims didn't use it, they
should have.

Braising benefits birds other than turkeys. Wild birds
that you shoot on the wing may be tough, and braising
will tenderize them. Domesticated game birds such as
farm-raised pheasant and squab, although tender, are
often dull and lacking the flavor that braising can impart.
Today's market pheasant often tastes like dried-out chicken
unless cooked with a moisturizing accompaniment like
sauerkraut, turnips, or leeks. Harking back to the medie-

val and Renaissance tradition of game pies, the Scots are still fond of pheasant and leek pies. Jane Grigson furnishes one of these pies from the town of Gullane in her *British Cookery* (1984), and I've adapted her recipe here, without the pastry, by braising pheasants on a bed of leeks.

Our native wild quail, or bobwhite, often miscalled partridge, has long been replaced in our markets by farm-raised varieties of quail with names like Pharaoh, Egyptian, or Japanese, names as exotic as the originally misnamed Turkie-cock or *coq d'Inde*. Because these quail are tiny, they are best cooked quickly, by roasting, grilling, or sautéing. Here I've sautéed them and nested them on a salad, from which they should be plucked and eaten, like all little birds, with fingers and not with forks. Sautéed separately, the recipe for popcorn stuffing, with the addition of some wild mushrooms perhaps, would also provide a good nest for quail.

Brillat-Savarin, after his famous turkey hunt in the woods near Hartford, Connecticut, in the early nineteenth century, braised his quail, or partridge, *en papillote*, and his gray squirrels in Madeira. As for the wild turkey he had shot, Brillat-Savarin confesses that where his thoughts might have been occupied with the speech of his American host in praise of independence and liberty, they were not. Instead, all the way home he had something quite different on his mind: "I was considering how best I should cook my turkey."

Braised Turkey with Popcorn Stuffing

One 7–10-pound turkey, wild or tame
4 cups popcorn stuffing (recipe follows)
salt and pepper to taste
¼ pound (1 stick) butter
2 carrots, chopped
1 onion, chopped
bay leaf, thyme, and parsley to taste
1 cup hot chicken broth
½ cup white wine

Lightly stuff the neck and rear cavities of the turkey and season the skin with salt and pepper. In a casserole with a lid, melt the butter and sauté carrots, onion, and seasonings about 5 minutes. Add the turkey, breast up, and baste it well with the butter and vegetables. Add hot broth and wine, cover tightly, and bake at 325° for 1½–1¾ hours, or until a meat thermometer registers 165°. Pour off broth and vegetables. Run turkey under the broiler a few minutes to brown the breast and thighs. Remove excess fat from the broth and puree broth and vegetables in a blender for the turkey gravy.

Serves 6–8.

Popcorn Stuffing

½ cup popcorn kernels
2 tablespoons oil
1 large onion, diced
3 stalks celery, diced

½ cup chopped parsley
¼ pound (1 stick) butter, melted
mixed sage, rosemary, thyme, salt, and pepper
   to taste

Pop the corn in hot oil in a large covered skillet. Grind the popped kernels in a food processor or food mill. Soften the onion, celery, and parsley in butter. Add the ground corn and season to taste.

Yields about 4 cups stuffing.

Braised Pheasant with Leeks

1 pair 2½–3-pound pheasants
2 tablespoons juniper berries
1 tablespoon black pepper
½ cup gin or scotch
6–8 large leeks
¼ pound (1 stick) butter
4 tablespoons olive oil
2 bay leaves
2 sprigs parsley
salt to taste
2 cups chicken broth
1 cup crème fraîche or heavy cream

Marinate the birds with the crushed juniper, pepper, and gin, covered and refrigerated, for 8 hours or overnight. Clean the leeks well, and chop the white part in a processor or by hand. Soften the leeks in a large casserole in half the butter for about 5 minutes. Pat the birds dry and brown them on all sides in the remaining butter, together with the oil, in a separate skillet. Put bay leaves and parsley in the cavities of each bird and salt their skins.

Place birds on top of the leeks. Heat broth in the browning skillet and scrape up the juices. Add the gin from the marinade and pour the broth over the birds. Cover tightly and braise in a 300° oven 1-1½ hours, or until birds are tender. Remove birds to a carving platter. Add crème fraîche or heavy cream to the leeks and reduce, if needed, until mixture is slightly thick. Serve carved birds on top of the leeks.

Serves 4-8.

Quail Salad

4 quail
flour for dusting
salt and pepper
3 tablespoons each butter and olive oil
½ pound wild mushrooms, such as shiitake
1 small red onion, chopped fine
2 cloves garlic, minced
1 cup finely chopped Italian parsley
rind of 2 lemons
1 radicchio, or 2 leaves red cabbage, shredded fine
1 bunch arugula

Butterfly the quail by splitting them down the back and spreading them open. Dust lightly with flour and season well with salt and pepper. Heat butter and oil in a large skillet and sauté quail, turning them to brown evenly, 10-12 minutes. Remove birds from the pan. Slice or chop mushrooms coarsely and sauté them quickly, 1-2 minutes, in the pan. Mix mushrooms with the onion, garlic, parsley, lemon rind, and radicchio, and place a mound of the mixture on 4 plates. Place a quail on top of each mound and circle with a few leaves of arugula.

Serves 4.

FROSTY BEAUTIES:
PUMPKINS AND PERSIMMONS

Were there a beauty contest for plants, pumpkins and persimmons would make an unlikely pair of contestants: the one a plump round matron, the other a delicate ripening nymphet. These are late bloomers who flame with the last of summer's sun and the first of winter's frost. Explorers called the pumpkin *pompion*, which meant a melon "cooked" by the sun, but indeed it ripens only in the fall. Captain John Smith, when he came upon persimmons in the wilds of Virginia in 1607, called them by their Indian name *pasiminan*, and noted the need for sun. "If it be not ripe it will draw a man's mouth awry with much torment," he wrote, "but when it is ripe it is as delicious as an apricock."

Settlers soon learned that it was not sun but frost that turned the mouth-puckering torment of an unripe persimmon into the deliciousness of an apricot. They also learned that pumpkins picked at the first frost will last through the winter. With either fruit, their beauty is more than skin deep and we should treat them more kindly than we do when we dump them into standard puddings and pies.

Our forebears learned from the Indians how to use these strange fruits in substantial stews and breads and in sauces for meat and fish. An English visitor to America in 1705 reported that she had "lodged at Stonington [Connecticut] and had Rost Beef and pumpkin sauce for supper." Indians, meanwhile, learned from the colonists how to use the pulp of both plants for brewing beer. It was only late in the nineteenth century that these many uses were straightened and corseted in a dully respectable persimmon pudding and a boring pumpkin pie.

The tastiest persimmon is our wild native type, which is small, oval, and burnt sienna in color. It is now making a sly comeback in specialty markets after having been displaced for over a century by Commodore Perry's favorites, those Japanese lovelies who today bear such names as Fuyu, Tamopan, or Hachiya. While the Japanese persimmon is larger and showier, it is also softer and blander than our red-skinned native.

To eat a ripe persimmon by peeling the skin back from the top to reveal a globe of matte velvet is an experience no pleasure seeker should forgo, but the season for ripeness is short. We can, however, puree the flesh and freeze it for later use. One use is to imitate the English method of turning fruit purees into "fools." Sweetened with honey and folded into heavy cream, persimmon puree makes a splendid persimmon fool. Another use we find in the American South, from the regional method of turning fruits and vegetables into "pones." In her *Savannah Cook Book* of 1933, Harriet Ross Colquitt adds a cup of persimmon pulp, after the first frost has sweetened the persimmons of northern Georgia, to a sweet potato pone. When grated raw, sweet potatoes (yet another orange-fleshed food) can make a delicious bread-cake, not unlike a carrot cake, and the persimmon provides natural sweetening.

Eating pumpkins, as opposed to decorative jack-o'-lantern types, are relatively small, firm-fleshed sugar pumpkin types with names like Big Max, Small Sugar, or Funny Face. The best of all eating pumpkins are the bright orange-fleshed West Indian pumpkins, or *calabaza*, once common in southern Florida but now imported to the States largely from the Caribbean.

Fresh, as opposed to canned, pumpkin puree is a revelation. Here I've put pumpkin puree into a standard yeast bread to make a punning showpiece for the Thanksgiving table. I mold the dough into a round pumpkin shape by letting it rise in a round ovenproof bowl. I then fit an actual pumpkin stem into the top of the dough just before baking.

We can best savor pumpkin flesh, however, not pureed but cubed, as they do in the Southwest when they add it to stews of chicken or lamb and flavor it with onions, chili, and pumpkin seeds. In the Far East, vegetarians mix cubed pumpkin and pumpkin seeds with lentils to make a perfectly balanced meal. As for the pumpkin seed itself, we have much to learn from Indians West and East about its values. Ground for sauces or toasted and salted for snacks, the green of a hulled pumpkin seed rivals the orange of pumpkin flesh for looks and taste.

Let Europeans breed hothouse plants. Americans go for well-rounded types that are as practical as they are glamorous. In any beauty contest judged by eaters, pumpkins and persimmons can back their show with substance.

Pumpkin Yeast Bread

1 cup pumpkin puree
1 package dry yeast
¼ cup warm water (110–115°)
4½–5 cups unbleached flour
2 tablespoons sugar
1 teaspoon salt
1 teaspoon pure ground chili (optional)
2 eggs, beaten
4 tablespoons butter, softened
½ cup toasted pumpkin seeds

To make puree cut a pumpkin in half and remove seeds and fibers. Cut each half in 3 or 4 pieces and bake at 350° for 1 hour. Scrape flesh from skin and puree in blender or food processor (a 3-pound pumpkin yields 3 cups of puree). To make dough, dissolve yeast in water and add to the pumpkin puree. Mix flour with sugar and seasonings and stir in the pumpkin, eggs, butter, and seeds. Knead 10 minutes by hand or 5 minutes by machine until dough is elastic. Let rise in a warm place until doubled (about 1-2 hours). Punch dough down and let rise again in a buttered round pot or ovenproof bowl (about 45 minutes). Bake at 375° for 35-40 minutes, or until bottom sounds hollow when tapped. Let cool on a rack.

Yields 1 large or 2 small loaves.

Pumpkin and Lentil Salad

1 small eating pumpkin (for 2 cups cubed
    pumpkin flesh)
2 tablespoons olive oil
1 large onion, chopped
1 sweet red bell pepper, seeded and chopped
1 clove garlic, minced
1 cup cooked lentils (green if possible)
Seasonings: 1 tablespoon grated ginger root,
    1 tablespoon lemon juice, 2 tablespoons minced
    parsley, 1/2 teaspoon salt, 1/4 teaspoon black
    pepper, 1/8 teaspoon ground cumin
1/2 cup toasted pumpkin seeds

Cut pumpkin in half, remove seeds and fibers, cut each half in several pieces, and pare outer skin. Cut flesh in 1/2-inch cubes. Heat oil in a large skillet and cook onion, pepper, and garlic 5 minutes. Add pumpkin, lentils, and seasonings. Cover skillet and cook gently 8–10 minutes, until pumpkin is just tender. Scrape into salad bowl, sprinkle with pumpkin seeds, and let cool to room temperature.

Serves 4–6.

Persimmon Sweet-Potato Pone

2 cups raw sweet potatoes, grated
½ cup brown sugar
¼ pound (1 stick) butter
¼ cup molasses
½ cup fresh orange juice
juice and grated rind of 1 orange
grated rind of 1 lemon
4 eggs, beaten
1 cup persimmon pulp
½ teaspoon each nutmeg, cloves,
  and cinnamon

Peel sweet potatoes and grate by hand or in food processor. Cream sugar with the butter and gradually beat in all remaining ingredients. Pour into a buttered baking dish (9 × 9 × 2) and bake at 325° for 1 hour. Cut in squares and serve warm.

Yields 9–16 squares.

Persimmon Fool

2 cups persimmon pulp (3–4 persimmons)
2 tablespoons lime or lemon juice
2 tablespoons dark honey
1 tablespoon dark rum
1 cup heavy cream

Cut a cross in the top of the persimmon and peel skin down enough to scrape out pulp with a spoon. Remove seeds. Mash pulp in a blender or food processor. Add lime juice, honey, and rum and taste for sweetness. Whip cream until stiff and fold into persimmon mixture.

Serves 4.

December

December

THE SCOTCH-IRISH SPUD

French Fries with Skin

Potato Caraway Wafers

Potatoes O'Brien

Potato Chocolate Torte

A BEEFEATER'S BEEF

Marinated Flank Steak

Beef Ragout with Wow-Wow Sauce

Hunter's Savory Salt Beef

Braised Short Ribs

CHRISTMAS DRIED FRUITS

Speckled Bread (*Bara Brith*)

Moroccan Lamb with Dates

Apricot-Almond Tart

Easy Tart Pastry

Brandied Prunes

THE SCOTCH-IRISH SPUD

Who does not love a mickey, a murphy, a spud? My Scotch-Irish family loved them at least once and often twice a day—baked, boiled, riced, mashed, fried, hashed, creamed, and scalloped. My family was innocent of the fact that spuds were not socially acceptable, here or abroad, until the eighteenth century, and often not even then.

Europeans were rightly suspicious of the strange knobby tuber Pizarro enthusiastically sent from Peru in 1540 as "a tasty, mealy truffle." Italians called it *tartufolie* and Germans *Kartoffel,* but as a truffle, the tuber didn't stand a chance. When Queen Elizabeth's cook prepared a dish of the new plant, he served her the leaves and tossed out the tuber. When Sir Francis Drake planted the tuber in Ireland, he wanted simply a cheap substitute for oats and barley. While my Presbyterian ancestors scorned Drake's religion, they ate his tubers and brought them along to Boston in 1708. But the potato had no cachet in America until Franklin and Jefferson discovered it in Paris and planted it in their own gardens.

Since then, the potato's status has been as vagrant as its uses. The potato lost respectability when Irish Catholics, after emigrating to America during the Potato Famine of 1845, survived on hot roasted "mickeys" and "murphies" bought from street vendors in Boston and New York. Today, however, the potato is something of a national symbol. The so-called French fry, of which Americans

consume 5 billion pounds a year, is as American as
McDonald's, and the baked potato has been transformed
by Pop artists like Claes Oldenburg into works of erotic
art.

Originally South American Indians ate potatoes raw
or baked them in the ashes of their campfires and hearths,
where the skins turned crisp and the insides mealy. They
were free from today's aluminum foil, which is a boon for
steaming tiny new potatoes but which ruins baking potatoes by keeping moisture in. The French took to frying
thin wafers of potatoes cut in fancy shapes. When they
sliced potatoes into rounds or scooped them into balls
they called them *à la française,* Pierre Blot tells us in his
1867 *Handbook of Practical Cookery.* When they cut
them in strips or "in pieces like carpels [pistils] of oranges"
(like shoestrings), they called them *à la Parisienne.*
American cooks like Sarah Josepha Hale adopted these
Frenchified shapes, cutting fries into corkscrews, ribbons,
and shavings, and sprinkling them with hot cayenne.

The English preferred to steam, boil, bake, or hash
potatoes. An ancestor of our corned beef hash was the
English "Lobscouse," a favorite with eighteenth-century
sailors who mixed potatoes with salt beef and onions.
Another descendant of English hash, which became popular in America in the 1930s, was Potatoes O'Brien, which
mixes diced or grated raw potatoes with red and green
peppers and Parmesan cheese. Because the starch in raw
potato binds whatever you mix with it, a potato pancake
the size of your frying pan makes the base for a fine
one-dish meal. One of my favorite mixtures is grated
potato with beef or pork cracklings, or leftover baked
potato skins fried crisp as cracklings, the whole fried in
beef or pork fat until crisply brown.

German-Jewish immigrants gave America both its
most practical and most exotic potato dishes, from blintzes
and knishes to desserts like Potato Chocolate Torte and

Potato Fluff Candy, found in Lizzie Kander's 1930 edition of *The Settlement Cookbook*. She includes among such delights a cocktail wafer of potato dough, deliciously flavored with caraway, and a startling combination of raw potatoes and unpeeled pears to accompany a roast chicken or roast pork. That should put the term *New* American Cuisine in its place.

The current nostalgia for home-style Americana has made even lumpy mashed potatoes a fad. As a lifelong masher, I shudder at this sort of potato abuse. America spent much of the nineteenth century devising potato hardware, such as potato beetles, riddles, pressers, ricers, and mashers, all designed to produce a light and fluffy potato puree misnamed "mash." One of my earliest kitchen privileges was to stand on a chair and work over a pot of boiled potatoes with a 1930s wooden-handled bent-metal masher. What cared I for the social status of a snowy mound indented carefully with the back of a spoon to form a hollow for a lake of melted butter? What more could a Calvinist heaven offer a lover of Irish spuds?

French Fries with Skin

Pick long, thin baking potatoes that you can cut in thick slices lengthwise with the skin on. Cut each potato in half lengthwise, lay flat side down and cut vertically. Pat the slices dry with paper towels. Heat beef fat or oil in a wok or deep skillet to 325° (hot but not smoking), and cook potatoes a handful at a time for about 5 minutes, or "until flabby but not colored," as James Beard says. Remove with slotted spoon and drain on paper towels. Leave at room temperature for an hour or more. When ready to serve them, reheat oil to 375° and refry potatoes quickly (2–4 minutes), until crisp and brown. Drain and salt.

Potato Caraway Wafers

1 cup boiled and riced potato (1 medium potato)
1/4 pound (1 stick) butter
1 cup unbleached flour
1 teaspoon salt
1/2 teaspoon black or white pepper
1 egg beaten with 1 tablespoon milk
1-2 tablespoons caraway seeds

Mix potatoes, while still warm, with butter. Mix in flour and salt and pepper lightly with a fork to form a dough. Wrap in plastic wrap and refrigerate for 60 minutes. Butter a flat baking sheet and roll or pat mixture 1/8 inch thick into a smooth square or rectangle. Brush top with egg and milk and sprinkle with caraway seeds. With a sharp knife, cut dough into narrow strips about 3 inches long. Bake at 350° for 10 minutes to dry the dough, then increase heat to 400° and bake 10 minutes more, or until wafers are crisp and brown.

Yields 3 dozen wafers.

Potatoes O'Brien

1 cup finely chopped red and green bell peppers
2 green onions, with tops, chopped fine
2 tablespoons minced parsley
2 cups raw grated potatoes
    (2 medium boiling potatoes)
½ cup freshly grated Parmesan cheese
salt, black pepper, and cayenne pepper to taste
4-6 tablespoons butter or beef or pork fat

In a food processor, chop the peppers, onions, and parsley together and set aside. Then grate the potatoes. Mix the vegetables, potatoes, seasonings, and cheese, and turn the mixture into a skillet of hot butter or fat (a cast-iron or nonstick skillet is best). Press the mixture flat with a spatula to form a large pancake. When the pancake is crisp and brown underneath (about 5 minutes), slide it onto a plate, then invert the plate over the skillet to brown the pancake on the other side.

Serves 2.

Potato Chocolate Torte

1¼ cups unblanched almonds
½ pound (2 sticks) butter
2 cups sugar
4 eggs, separated
1 cup all-purpose flour
2 teaspoons baking powder
1 teaspoon cinnamon
½ teaspoon ground cloves
4 ounces bittersweet chocolate, melted
1 cup cooked potatoes, riced
1 teaspoon vanilla extract
powdered sugar

Using a processor or grinder, grind the almonds fine but don't turn them into a paste. Cream the butter and sugar together, then add egg yolks, one at a time, and beat until fluffy. Mix together flour, baking powder, cinnamon, and cloves. Mix together lightly the chocolate, potatoes, and vanilla. Add the two mixtures alternately to the butter and sugar, then mix in the ground almonds. Beat the egg whites until stiff but not dry and fold them into the torte. Bake in a buttered 9-inch springform pan at 325° for 1½ hours. Cool on a rack. Sprinkle with powdered sugar when cold.

Serves 8–10.

A BEEFEATER'S BEEF

"Do not gnaw bones with your teeth, like a dog," Erasmus of Rotterdam advised his beef-eating friends in England four hundred years ago. "Pick them clean with the aid of a knife." A few centuries later beef-eating Americans were warned not to pick their teeth with a knife, but to keep the knife close to the bone. "If possible the knife should never be put in the mouth at all," the *Ladies' Indispensable Assistant* instructed ladies and gentlemen in New York in 1852, "and if at all, let the edges be turned outward."

Today, the problem for beef-eating Americans is not one of tooth-and-knife table manners, but one of cost. The question is not "Where's the beef?" but "Where's the money?" Let's look to the original British beefeaters, however, who gave us not only our costly beef-eating habits, but also beef-cooking traditions that spare money fears for the cook and knife fears for the eater. Four of these beef-cooking ways were standard in Anglo-American cookbooks until our own century, when beef cuts that saved time began to replace beef cuts that saved money.

One of the simplest English ways with cheaper cuts of beef was to turn a flank steak, that thin muscular strip along a cow's belly, into a London broil. Eighteenth- and nineteenth-century cooks rolled and tied this strip to make a "collared beef." They would rub the muscle with salt and either sugar or treacle to tenderize it, then roll it up like a gentleman's collar, tie it in a cloth, and boil it like a pudding. Today, Americans as well as Londoners simply broil the meat after marinating it in olive oil (to make up for the lack of fat) and lemon juice and soy sauce (to tenderize and flavor it). The cook can spare the diner any embarrassing knife work by carving the beef across the grain in thin slices.

The English applied a similar salt-and-sugar tenderizer to a hefty boneless cut like beef round or rump to make "hunter's beef," so named for its additional strong flavoring agents like juniper berries, often associated with game. Hunter's beef is a remarkable salted and spiced beef that is still common in the American South and should be known elsewhere because it is as practical as it is tasty.

Dr. William Kitchiner, in his 1831 edition of *The Cook's Oracle*, "Adapted to the American Public by a Medical Gentleman of England," recommends a good shin of beef, stewed. But he advises the mistress of the table to call it "ragout beef," for, as he explains, "the homely appellation of 'shin of beef stewed,' is enough to give your genteel eater the locked jaw." Evidently even beef ragout lacked a certain something for your genteel eater, since Kitchiner directs the cook to "Send up Wow-wow sauce in a boat." The sauce, which calls for pickled cucumbers or walnuts, plus mushroom catchup, burnet vinegar, and other piquant ingredients, may be one of the progenitors of American chow-chow pickles, with their thick flour-based mustard and vinegar sauce. At any rate, you can make your beef as wow-wow as you choose.

Dr. Kitchiner mentions his "Hunter's Savoury Salt Beef" as "deserving the particular attention of those families who frequently have accidental customers dropping in at luncheon or supper."

One of my favorite beef cuts, I confess, does bring up the knife problem again because the flavor comes from fat and bone. Beef short ribs, which the butcher cuts from a large rib roast, are always a good buy for economy combined with flavor. I rub the ribs with herbs and garlic, spice them with Worcestershire or Tabasco sauce, and braise them in a good beef broth (sometimes with vegetables like carrots and onions and potatoes) to make a rib-sticking meal that I serve to my very best friends. For company I slice the beef from the bone before serving. When alone, however, I gnaw those delicious bones with my teeth, as happy as any dog.

Marinated Flank Steak

One 1½-2-pound flank steak
¼ cup minced green onions
1 tablespoon minced ginger root
¼ cup olive oil
juice of ½ lemon
1 tablespoon soy sauce (mushroom soy preferred)
½ teaspoon black pepper

Marinate meat in the combined ingredients in a covered bowl or plastic bag in the refrigerator for 6-24 hours. Broil as close to the flame as possible, 2 to 3 minutes per side, to sear the outside and keep the inside rare. Cut across the grain at an angle to make slices about 3 inches wide and ⅛ inch thick.
Serves 3-4.

Beef Ragout with Wow-Wow Sauce

2 pounds boneless shin of beef, or other
   stew beef
salt and pepper to taste
flour, for dredging
2 tablespoons oil
1 cup beef broth
3 sprigs parsley
2 sprigs fresh thyme
2 bay leaves
1 teaspoon allspice berries, crushed
1/2 cup each chopped onion, carrot,
   and celery

Cut the meat in 2-inch cubes, season them with salt and pepper, and roll them in the flour. Heat the oil in a skillet or casserole and brown the beef quickly on all sides. Add broth, herbs, and allspice berries, cover with a lid, and let liquid barely simmer 2–2 1/2 hours. Add the chopped vegetables and simmer another 30 minutes, or until meat is tender. Serve with Wow-Wow Sauce.
    Serves 4.

FOR THE SAUCE:
3 tablespoons butter
1 tablespoon flour
1 cup hot beef broth
1 teaspoon Dijon mustard
1 tablespoon wine vinegar
1 tablespoon capers
1/2 cup minced parsley
1/4 cup chopped dill pickles

Melt butter in a saucepan, add the flour, and cook, stirring, 2–3 minutes. Remove from heat and stir in the broth. Bring to a simmer and add remaining ingredients. Pour sauce over the beef.

Yields about 1½ cups sauce.

Hunter's Savory Salt Beef

One 5-pound rump or round roast
½ cup kosher salt
¼ cup brown sugar
2 tablespoons black peppercorns
4 bay leaves
1 tablespoon allspice berries
2 tablespoons juniper berries
½ cup beef broth

Remove fat and skin from the outside of the roast. Grind all the seasonings together in a blender and rub them well into the beef. Put the beef in a plastic bag, tie it, and keep refrigerated 7–10 days, turning the bag over every other day so the brine soaks in evenly. When ready to cook, remove meat from the marinade, wrap it in foil with the beef broth for liquid, and put the foil package in a covered casserole to braise. Bake in a 290° oven for 2 hours. Remove from oven, turn the package over, and let the meat cool in its own juice. When the beef is cool, press it with a board weighted with a heavy can and refrigerate it overnight. Keep refrigerated until ready to use. Slice paper thin and serve at room temperature.

Serves 10–15.

Braised Short Ribs

2 pounds short ribs

2 cloves garlic, mashed

Seasonings: 1 teaspoon salt; 1/2 teaspoon black
    pepper; 1/4 teaspoon each sage, rosemary,
    and thyme; 1 large dash Worcestershire or
    Tabasco sauce

3/4 cup beef broth

Optional: 4 cups chopped vegetables such as
    carrots, turnips, leeks, onions, and potatoes

freshly grated horseradish

Rub meat with garlic and seasonings. Broil meat
about 5 minutes per side until well seared. Place in a
baking dish with boiling hot broth, cover tightly, and
braise at 300° for about 1½ hours or until meat is fork
tender. (Add optional vegetables the last half hour, and
add more salt, if desired.) Cut meat from the bone and
carve crosswise in thick slices. Serve with grated, fresh
horseradish.

Serves 3-4.

CHRISTMAS DRIED FRUITS

The plum Jack Horner thumbed from his Christmas mince pie had no more to do with plums, or prunes, than had the Christmas plum pudding that Bob Cratchit declared "the greatest success achieved by Mrs. Cratchit since their marriage." So ancient is the use of dried fruits in festal winter dishes that the English names for these fruits have become as minced as the ingredients of English pottages, puddings, and pies.

"Plums" in Christmas plum puddings are neither plums nor prunes, but raisins and currants. England's medieval pottages, which combined meats or fish with dried fruits and exotic spices, relied heavily on raisins and currants because they were the cheapest of imported fruits. When wealthy Elizabethans began to upgrade their Christmas pottages by importing prunes from Spain and France, the word "plum" gave class to stews and puddings that had naught but raisins and currants. To compound confusion, if "plum" usually meant raisin, so too did the word "currant." "Dried currants" bear no relation to the red, white, and black berries of the currant bush that make jelly for the English and crème de cassis for the French. In the context of dried fruits, currants are very small raisins originally imported from Greece, where the name "raisins of Corinth" was corrupted to "currant."

Englishmen had no reason to distinguish names or fruits too nicely, as all

manner of fruits, fresh and dried, went into their puddings for flavor and nutrition. When John Josselyn wrote
An Account of Two Voyages to New England (1674), he
encountered Massachusetts Indians gathering wild berries to mix "into Indian boyling Puddings, for variety in
the English manner." So too Jacques Cartier discovered
Canadian Indians cultivating plums and drying them in
order to have a supply of prunes for winter stews.

Sun-drying is the oldest form of preserving, but when
sugar became cheap enough for common use, fruits were
often candied as well as dried. *The Cook's Own Book*
(1832), "by a Boston Housekeeper," instructs fellow housekeepers to dry apricots by first cooking them in syrup,
then putting the stewed fruit upon dishes to dry "in the
sun under garden glasses."

Few Bostonians today would bother to dry apricots,
since the sun in California does that for them. Ancient
Persians called apricots "sun eggs" and Spanish mission
fathers, as early as the eighteenth century, found the
sun of California congenial for apricots, along with figs
and dates. As a California child, I took such fruits for
granted, not knowing that California had become the
principal source of dried fruits for all of the States and
much of the world. So abundant were these fruits in our
backyard that I assumed everybody squished ripe apricots between their toes in summer and threw green dates
in winter, to annoy passing motorists, the way children
elsewhere might throw snowballs.

Through its dried fruits, California links ancient Persia
to medieval England and modern Morocco. Any dried
fruit is a gift of the sun that intensifies its flavor, so
that to eat a nugget of dried fruit in a bread, a
stew, or a tart is to eat a nugget of sunshine in
the midst of winter's barrenness. That must
be why the Welsh created a bread they
call *Bara Brith,* or speckled bread,

flavored with saffron, allspice, and nutmeg and speckled with raisins, currants, and apricots. The bread was a favorite of Cornish miners who worked the lead mines of North Cardiganshire at the beginning of this century and who needed all the sunshine they could get.

Blessed or cursed with an excess of sun, Moroccans continue even now the medieval tradition of mixing fruits and meats in the stew they call *tagine*. Some of the best combinations are the most unlikely: lamb with dried apricots or, as I've done here, lamb with dried dates.

Dried fruits go with nuts, particularly apricots with almonds. Since the apricot kernel has the flavor of bitter almonds, traditionally the pitted apricot fruit was preserved with a few crushed kernels to supply that flavor. In my tart recipe I've combined three of my favorite flavors—apricots, almonds, and raspberries—with one of my favorite textures, the delectably creamy cheese called *mascarpone*.

To redeem the reputation of dried prunes, too long associated with the pharmacy rather than the kitchen, I've plumped prunes with brandy (as one might do figs) to mix with tart grapefruit sections or to spoon over vanilla ice cream. Martha Washington, in her *Booke of Cookery* (1749), put prunes in a "Plumb Broth" made of beef or marrow bones, bread, sugar, raisins, and currants and colored with sandalwood. This was the upgraded medieval pottage that evolved into Christmas pudding. Perhaps Martha's husband, George, at some Christmas feast, honored the prune in Martha's broth by declaring it "the greatest success achieved by Mrs. Washington since their marriage."

Speckled Bread
(Bara Brith)

1 cup milk
¼ teaspoon each saffron, cinnamon, allspice,
    and nutmeg
2 tablespoons brown sugar
1 package dry yeast
2 cups unbleached flour
1 cup whole-wheat flour
1½ teaspoons salt
2 tablespoons softened butter
⅓ cup each currants, golden raisins, and
    dried apricots

Heat milk with the spices and sugar until warm enough (105°–115°) to dissolve the yeast. Remove from heat and add yeast. Mix the two flours with salt and butter and stir in the yeast mixture. Chop the apricots coarsely and add all the dried fruits to the dough. Knead dough until elastic and glossy, then let rise until doubled. Punch dough down with your fist, place it in a buttered loaf pan (9 × 4 × 4), and let it rise again. Bake at 375° about 35–40 minutes.

    Yields 1 loaf.

Moroccan Lamb with Dates

3 pounds lamb meat
1 teaspoon each salt and black pepper
pinch of saffron
⅛ teaspoon cayenne pepper

1 tablespoon grated ginger root
2 cloves garlic, minced
3 tablespoons olive oil
1 cup minced onions
3 cups hot chicken broth
1 cup (½ pound) pitted dates
2 tablespoons fresh coriander
cinnamon

Trim lamb of fat and cut in 1½-inch cubes. Mix seasonings with ginger and garlic and heat gently in olive oil in a casserole. Toss the cubed lamb in the spiced oil, add half the onions, pour in the broth, and simmer for 1½-2 hours. Add remaining onions, dates, and coriander and simmer 15-20 minutes, or until lamb is tender. Sprinkle with cinnamon just before serving.

Serves 6.

Apricot-Almond Tart

1 cup dried apricots
½ cup dark rum
½ cup raspberry jam
One prebaked 9-inch tart shell (recipe follows)
¾ cup mascarpone (or other fresh
    triple-cream cheese)
⅓ cup slivered almonds, toasted

Put apricots in a small pan, and add rum and water to barely cover. Stew gently until liquid is nearly evaporated. Cool. Spread jam evenly over the bottom of the tart shell. Cover jam with the mascarpone, cover this with the apricots, and top with the almonds.

Serves 6-8.

Easy Tart Pastry

½ cup cream cheese, softened·
½ cup (2 sticks) butter, softened
1½ cups all-purpose flour
2 tablespoons sugar
½ teaspoon salt

Whip cream cheese with the butter. Mix together flour, sugar, and salt, then mix lightly with the butter and cheese mixture. Chill dough 30 minutes, then pat onto the bottom and sides of a tart or pie pan. If you don't mind the tart shrinking, you needn't line the pastry with foil and beans or other weights. Bake at 325° for 25–35 minutes. Let cool.

Yields one 9-inch shell.

Brandied Prunes

2-inch piece of vanilla bean
¾ pound pitted prunes
2–4 slices ginger root, minced
½ cup cognac
¼ cup honey
½ cup strong black coffee

Split the vanilla bean into quarters and combine with the remaining ingredients. Place them in a pint jar with a tight lid. Let stand in a cool place for 2 weeks, turning the jar upside down occasionally to keep the prunes immersed.

Serves 4–8.

Bread

Bread for All Seasons

YEAST BREADS

Sourdough Country Bread from Scratch

Walnut-Oat Bread

Sprouted Wheat Bread

Tuscan Herb Bread (*Focaccia*)

QUICK BREADS

American Egg Corn Pone

Scottish Oatcakes

English Cream Scones

Irish Whole-Wheat Soda Bread

Finnish Barley Bread

YEAST BREADS

"To make good bread," *The Buckeye Cookbook* of 1883 instructs us, "always be 'Up in the morning early, just at the peep of day,'" in order to compensate for the weather. In winter the flour had to be warmed, and in summer the yeast had to be kept from going sour. In the days when home baking was a necessity conditioned by time and the weather, good bread was as hard to find as a good man or a good cigar.

Readers of *The Buckeye Cookbook* must have envied the European who bought her loaf from the village baker. The American villager had to bake her own, in whatever pot, griddle, lard bucket, or oven she had at hand. An American villager had to deal with flour that was coarse, unbolted, rancid, and often infested with marauders like the meal moth, "far more to be dreaded than rats or mice." An American had to make her yeast from scratch — from hops, malt, rye, potatoes, or molasses — and once the ferment was corked, she was lucky if the yeast did not sour or explode. An American had to heat her oven with fagots or brush that might overheat it and scorch her loaves, to prevent which she was advised to "wet an old broom two or three times, and turn it round near the top of the oven till it dries."

Once the nineteenth-century home baker had conquered the hazards of flour, yeast, and heat, she had to face not only changes in the weather, but the children and the cow down sick and Pa home drunk and the well run dry. As often as not her loaf was sour, heavy, ill-baked, indigestible, unpalatable, unwholesome, and mildewed before the week was out. "These accidents so frequently happen when bread is made at home by careless, unpracticed or incompetent persons," Miss Eliza Leslie wrote in her *Directions for Cookery* in 1837, "that families who live in cities or towns will generally risk less and save more by obtaining their bread from a professional baker."

No wonder twentieth-century Americans embraced with joy that airy, all-white, long-lasting, sterilized, factory-made loaf that we find today preserved in cellophane coffins and laid to rest in supermarket morgues. When 99 percent of American bread was made at home—and it was so made until the second decade of this century —Miss Leslie could hardly anticipate that one day most commercially made bread would be indistinguish-able from the product housewives are now warned not to squeeze.

Fortunately, to make good bread at home today is far easier and far more fun than in the days when ingredients were as unreliable as the weather. Bread is in every sense elemental, with its essential grain, liquid, leavening, and heat derived from the four elements of earth, water, air, and fire. Today we can get good flours, good liquids, good yeast, and controlled heat that defy variable weather. All we lack is the crucial element of time. But once we understand the rhythm of bread making and the need to give yeast its own good time to ripen and grow, to make bread at all is to make good bread. Ripening time is the chief conditioner of a loaf's taste; it is also essential in determining the other qualities of volume, texture, and keeping power. Speed is the enemy of bread leavened by yeast. Given time and under-standing, however, yeast performs wonders and the levitating powers of yeast can make magicians of us all.

FLOUR

No bread is better than the kind or quality of its grain. In America the most common grains are corn (or maize), wheat, rye, barley, and oats. Wheat is the primary grain for yeast-leavened bread because wheat contains the highest amount of gluten. Gluten is a protein that determines how well a flour can glue itself together into an elastic web. The web swells like a balloon from the bubbles of carbon dioxide generated by the leaven.

Gluten therefore determines the volume and texture of breads. At the bottom of the gluten scale is corn, which has no gluten at all. The breads of the American Indians, made of a corn-and-water paste, were as flat and thin as their hearthstones. Next to corn are oats, which are so low in gluten that they bake best in a flat cake unless mixed with glutenous wheat. Barley is similar to oats, with the added disadvantage of a gray color. Rye has a moderate gluten content and can stand on its own, although the rye loaf will be compact and dense. At the top of the gluten scale is wheat of two kinds: soft and hard. Soft wheat, of 4 to 5 percent gluten, is the kind of wheat England and the colonists grew. Now it is used chiefly for cakes and pastries and for mixing with the "strong" flour of hard wheat, which is 18 to 19 percent gluten.

Thousands of years ago man learned to grind grain into meal and meal into flour, so that bread is one of our earliest "processed" foods. Its long history has been one of ever-increasing refinement. Our very word "flour," derived from the French *fleur* and meaning "the flower of meal," suggests delicacy and refinement. Until the middle of the last century, millers had always crushed grain between

rotating millstones to produce stone-ground meal of vary-
ing coarseness. Crushing the grain separated the bran
(or husk) from the inner kernel, which contains both the
starchy endosperm and the germ, that minute embryo
that is the life of each individual grain. The miller would
then sift the meal through a bolting cloth of canvas, linen,
or silk gauze in order to eliminate as much of the bran as
possible.

In the 1840s the invention of rollers, made first of
porcelain and then of steel, revolutionized the milling of
grain. Instead of crushing grain, the rollers split it open,
shearing the endosperm from both bran and germ. Bakers
rejoiced because coarse bran cut the gluten and reduced
the volume of a baked loaf. Bakers, millers, and store-
keepers rejoiced because the oil in wheat germ turned
flour rancid. Bran and germ together were made into
animal feed, and the remaining endosperm was pulverized and bleached to make a finer, whiter flour.

Bleaching occurs naturally when milled grain oxi-
dizes and matures, to the improvement of color and flavor
unless the grain is kept so long that it becomes stale.
Millers soon discovered that bleaching with either agene
or chlorine gas would both speed the maturing process
and delay decay. Since whiteness, volume, and shelf life
were the priorities of professional bakers, they opted for
the stripped, bleached flour that once signified progress
and upward mobility. When nutritionists squawked at
the loss of vitamins and minerals, these nutrients were
artificially restored. But the living germ that gave flavor,
color, and character to wheat was lost. Until recently, we
had to buy wheat germ separately and add it ourselves to
flour that was literally lifeless.

Luckily, the health-food generation of the 1960s and
1970s demanded more nutritious fare, and a
greater variety of flours is now avail-

able to the home baker, along with all-bran meal and wheat germ. So effective have the health foodists been that most supermarkets today carry a number of wheat flours, and even a bread flour, in addition to the standard white, bleached, all-purpose flour.

All-purpose flour is about 12 percent gluten from a mixture of hard and soft wheat, to serve the triple purposes of bread, cake, and pastry making. *Bread flour* contains a higher proportion of hard wheat in order to provide more gluten for bread making. *Unbleached flour* has more flavor than bleached flour and is a lovely creamy color, but it still lacks the germ. *Whole-wheat flour*, once called graham flour after food reformer Dr. Sylvester Graham, who preached the virtues of bran in purging human plumbing of poisons and wastes, contains the full grain with bran and germ. These two elements account for most of the fiber, oil, and vitamin B content of the grain, plus a quarter of its protein. The more fiber, however, the less these nutrients are able to be absorbed by the body, so that some removal of bran is desirable. *Whole meal* is the English version of whole-wheat flour, in which some 15 percent of the bran has been extracted to make a lighter and more digestible loaf.

Home bakers today can mill their own flours in an electric grinder or, more coarsely, in a food processor. Wheat grains do vary enormously in quality, and therefore in taste, depending on the soil and water and weather in which they're grown. As Karen Hess, a noted food writer and bread maker, says, "There are *crus* and vintages in wheat, just as in wines," in countries such as France that take their bread seriously. If you can buy high-quality wheat kernels of guaranteed freshness, then grinding your own meal and flour is as efficacious as grinding your own coffee from freshly roasted beans. From my local health food stores, I am able to get a good supply of whole kerneled grains, of hard and soft wheat, of oats and rye, which I can grind or sprout or soak or use whole, to vary texture and flavor in the endless experimentation that makes bread making fun.

YEAST

It's odd to realize that yeast-leavened bread is a "brew" that depends upon the same kind of fermentation that turns grapes to wine and grains to malt. Yeast is a living plant "of the fungus tribe," as Mrs. Mary Lincoln of the famed Boston Cooking School called it. Until late in the nineteenth century, brewing had always been as much of a country housewife's duty as baking. In rural America the home baker usually had to brew her own yeast to make both bread and beer.

Yeasts are single-celled plants that proliferate by feeding on starch or sugar, both of which naturally ferment when they are wet and warm. The growing yeast buds break off to create more buds, so that a single tablespoon of dry yeast, which contains initially about 130 billion cells, will double that number in a couple of hours if it has wet flour to feed on in a warm place. In the process the cells give off carbon dioxide, which swells the elastic web of gluten to make dough rise.[*]

The prepackaged, air-dried yeast granules of today's supermarket would have delighted the home bakers and brewers of a century ago, who were constantly frustrated by yeast gone sour and impotent. Yeast was most commonly grown on mixtures of bran mash, molasses, potatoes,

[*]For a detailed scientific explanation of how yeast works on dough, see Harold McGee's *On Food and Cooking: The Science and Lore of the Kitchen* (1984). The electron microscope photographs, as well as the text, are remarkable.

and even pumpkins. Hops were frequently added both to sweeten and to stabilize these ferments, which were apt to be bitter and certain to be temperamental in their potency. Once brewed, the yeast had to be preserved. Sometimes it was bottled and sometimes dried, either in cakes or in thin sheets that had been spread in successive layers on a board.

By the middle of the nineteenth century, professional bakers began to develop a more refined and reliable product than the yeast made by professional brewers from malt-based liquors. (The nutritional yeast sold in health food stores today under the label brewer's yeast is not a leavening yeast at all and can't be used for bread making or brewing.) About the same time, *compressed yeast* was introduced into England from Holland by experimenters who had long sought a means to turn liquid yeast solid. They found that when water was extracted from yeast "cream," flakes were produced that could be compressed into cakes. This partially dried yeast keeps best in the freezer, and when it is dissolved in liquid it is sluggish until fed the sugar supply that will make it bubble. A spoonful or two of granulated sugar hastens its action and proves that the yeast is still potent. The addition of sugar to the American bread loaf in the second half of the nineteenth century was one result of the new processing of yeast.

Today's dried yeast granules work slightly differently. Although dried yeast stores well at room temperature (it also keeps best in the freezer), that convenience is offset by the fact that it demands liquid of a fairly exact temperature before it begins to work. It will bubble without any source of sugar, but it requires an optimum temperature of between 105° and 110° to develop its full potency. The most recent development of yeast processing, *instant yeast* (with brand names like Rapid Rise and Quick-Rise), is designed to eliminate this first step of dissolving the granules in a hot but not too hot liquid before adding them to the flour.

Some claim to find a difference in taste in dough made with solid yeast cakes instead of granules, and now no doubt with yesterday's dried granules instead of today's instant ones, but I find none. Baker's yeasts today are grown from a solution of molasses and water, and it's not the difference in yeast processing that determines flavor but the amount of time and the kind of conditions under which the yeast works on the flour.

As the germ is the life of a wheat kernel, so yeast is the life of a ripened dough. It's the speed with which the yeast converts the carbohydrates of flour to sugar that affects the taste of a baked loaf and gives it specific character. The growth of the yeast can be speeded or slowed, according to need. Once activated, yeast works quickly under warm conditions and slowly under cold. High temperatures will stop its growth altogether (130° F for compressed yeast and 140° for yeast granules). If you want to delay the action of yeast, you can put bread dough in the refrigerator overnight. If you want to speed its action, you can put bread dough over a pilot light or under a hot electric light, such as an oven light. Sugar speeds the action of yeast, while salt slows it. Therefore, if you are using a sweetener, add the sugar first and the salt later.

In the days of unreliable yeasts, the home baker usually began her bread making with a mixture of liquid, yeast, and flour. If she could get no yeast from baker or brewer, she would make a "starter" of flour and water or milk, which she would let stand for several days, allowing wild yeasts to develop, before she added more flour to the starter in order to make a "sponge." A starter was the first step in making the bread we call "sourdough," for the fermentation of flour by wild yeasts is so slow that sourness is an inevitable result. The second step was to make a sponge of this fermenting mix by adding more flour to feed the burgeoning yeast and develop its power three- or four-fold. In addition to sourdough white or whole-wheat breads, rye breads are usually made with a fermenting sponge to give them more taste and to increase the power of yeast on low-gluten flour.

When commercial compressed yeast became available, the home baker would still have to test, or "proof," the yeast to make sure it was still good. With today's dried yeast, the dated packages indicate the life span of the granules so that proofing isn't necessary. You can, in fact, add the granules directly to the flour, as with instant yeast; but with dried yeast, to get it going, the added liquid needs to be at a higher temperature, 120° to 130°F. Temperatures are hard to gauge without a thermometer, and I find that the most useful one is a small pocket thermometer of the kind used for microwave ovens.

LIQUIDS AND FLAVORINGS

Liquid of some kind is necessary to turn the flour to paste. With wheat flour the proteins of the endosperm mix with water, or other liquid, to create the gluten that will make the dough plastic and elastic. The kind of liquid used will affect the texture, flavor, and keeping power of the baked loaf. The standard French and Italian loaf uses only water for its liquid and salt for its flavor. The standard English or American loaf is more apt to use some form of milk for its liquid and some kind of sweetening, along with salt, for its flavor. Dairy liquids with a high fat content, like sweet or sour cream, buttermilk, or yoghurt, will produce a fine crumb from the increased fat content. Many recipes will call for milk and butter, which serve the same purpose as rich cream. Sometimes a dairy solid, such as cheese, is added. Cheese supplies not only flavor and protein substance, but also additional fat.

Fat of any kind alters texture by making the crumb tender and tight instead of open and chewy. Fat also, whether butter, lard, vegetable shortening, vegetable oil, or nut oil, helps to preserve a loaf by keeping it moist. Since fat coats the gas cells in the risen dough, it can help increase and maintain volume, but too much fat can break down the cells and make the loaf dense and heavy. How much is too much? With bread, everything depends upon proportion. Hard wheat will absorb more water than soft wheat, since the gluten proteins will absorb about twice their weight in water. The humidity and temperature of the air, as well as the temperature of the flour and liquids, also affect the absorptive powers of the flour. That is why bread recipes often call for a minimum amount of flour, to which more is added during the kneading to make the dough optimally elastic and glossy. That is why bread recipes cannot be exact. The best rule is to experiment — and keep on experimenting.

Eggs are sometimes added, as part of the liquid, to make a bread richer in color and taste and higher in volume, since the leavening powers of a whole egg augment the leavening powers of yeast. Other liquids are sometimes added for more exotic flavorings and colorings: beer, coffee, tomato juice, zucchini juice, coconut milk, orange juice, carrot juice. The absorptive powers of flour make the use of such liquids more plausible than one might think, turning bright red tomato juice, for example, into a pale and delicate pink.

The use of other flavorings, like salt and sweeteners, depends entirely on individual taste. From the time man first discovered salt, he added it to his bread to increase the loaf's savor. Sweetening, on the other hand, was seldom used except for festal breads. Not until the nineteenth century, and then only in England among European countries, did sugar become a standard component of the daily loaf. Perhaps the chief reason for this was that England's industrial processing of refined white sugar coincided with the new industrial processing of refined, bleached flour, to the sorrow of subsequent generations of nutritionists. The less industrialized continent resolutely resisted England's new factory loaf. Since the American loaf was based on the English, it too increased its sweeteners, conditioning modern palates to find unsweetened bread tasteless. Unfortunately, even health foodists who programmatically scorn refined white sugar will add quantities of honey and molasses to their "all-natural" loaves. Fortunately, however, as more Americans sample at home and abroad the infinite variety of the world's unsweetened breads, ranging from the *pita* loaves of the Near and Far East to the *chapati* of India and the black breads of Russia, we no longer demand the soft, white sugared loaf of our grandparents and great-grandparents.

KNEADING AND RISING

Kneading is the process that aerates the dough and develops the gluten. Punching, folding, and slapping the dough about activate the gluten and develop it, an exercise that is healthy for both the dough and the baker. "Spend at least twenty minutes—half an hour is better—in this kind of useful gymnastics," Marion Harland advised in her *Common Sense in the Household* (1871), in order to produce dough that "rebounds like India-rubber after a smart blow of the fist." Current recipes are apt to say, "until the dough is silky and elastic."

The twenty minutes advised by Mrs. Harland are for large amounts of dough in a relatively cold kitchen. Ten minutes by hand are usually enough to turn the sticky, lumpy flour into a smooth and springy ball. The usual method of kneading by hand is to push the dough down and away from you with the heel of one or both hands, then to fold the dough back toward you, and finally to turn it a quarter of a circle before repeating. The pleasure of kneading is to establish a rhythm of push, fold, and turn (on a floured or cold surface like marble) until the dough sticks to itself and springs back into shape when pushed. You can slap the dough vigorously onto the counter or board, or smash it with your fist. At this stage no kind of violence can harm it and some may do it good.

The professional baker uses a power-driven mixer and kneader to make bread in quantity. The nineteenth-century home baker often used hand-cranked bread buckets for kneading, just as today's home baker can use a heavy-duty electric mixer equipped with a dough hook. Today's baker can also mix and knead with a food processor, but only in small batches. With an electric mixer you knead the dough until it forms a knot around the hook. With a processor, the kneaded dough will begin to form a bouncing ball.

What the hand will do in ten minutes or more the mixer will do in five, and the processor in one. Machines are apt to produce a finer, cakelike texture because they are more efficient in aerating the dough uniformly than even the strongest hands are. With sticky doughs like rye or egg breads, the machine often has a distinct advantage in handling the dough. In using a processor, however, you must be careful not to overknead and end up with a sticky, inelastic dough. Many like to knead briefly first by machine and then by hand, not only for the pleasure of feeling the living, silken dough take shape, but also for better control.

Once the gluten is fully developed, the yeast needs time and warmth to blow the bubbles that will stretch the protein web and cause the dough to rise. You can vary the time and number of risings according to your convenience, remembering always that time is the key to flavor. The usual formula is to let the dough rise in a warm place (between 70° and 80°) so that it will double in volume in about an hour and a half. A good way to produce draft-free constant warmth in a cold kitchen is to put the dough into an oven that is warmed by a pan of hot or boiling water. The oven light of an electric oven provides further warmth if you want speedier rising. In any case, you should cover the container of dough with plastic or a towel, or both, because yeast likes steamy warmth. While an American home baker will often put the dough inside a plastic bag, with the air squeezed out to allow room for the dough's doubling, a French baker traditionally wraps his dough in swaddling clothes. That is, he covers the dough with cheesecloth in a basket, then encloses the basket within a large air-filled plastic bag within a blanket. The basket allows the yeast to breathe within its plastic bubble.

To test whether the dough has risen sufficiently, press two fingers in the top, and if the dough remains indented, the gluten has been stretched to its limit. Some breads, such as pizza doughs, require only one rising. Other breads, particularly those with hard wheat flours, require a second rising to more fully develop the gluten and flavor. For a second rising, you punch the risen dough down with your fist to deflate it before letting it rise again. A second rising takes about half the time of the first, around forty-five minutes. Some breads take a third rising to develop a finer crumb and a more distinctive flavor.

The flexibility of yeast growth allows you to refrigerate a kneaded dough to slow its rising; you can even freeze the dough and bring it again to room temperature.

To speed a dough's rising, you can double the amount of yeast or let it rise in temperatures as high as 95° F. *But* high heat can develop a sourish taste in the dough and excess yeast can obtrude with a yeasty taste.

To shape the dough into loaves after the first or second rising, you can help the gluten create an unbroken skin by first patting the dough into a flat circle, then folding the dough in half over on itself, and "seaming" it with the heels of your hands. If you are using a loaf pan, round the two ends of the dough toward the seam and place the loaf in the pan seam side down. If you are making round loaves to place on a baking sheet or tile, first flatten the dough and then round the edges under in order to shape the dough into a high ball, which will spread somewhat as it expands. If you are making long French or Italian loaves, you stretch the dough into ropes by rolling each rope with the heels of your hands. Such loaves are usually slashed diagonally across the top to control breaks in the crust that occur when the dough expands in the baking.

BAKING

The high heat of the oven stops the yeast from further growth and thus preserves the shape of the previously risen loaf. The kind of heat, dry or wet, determines the relation of crust to crumb. Steam, at the beginning of the baking, creates the best crust. The old-fashioned bake oven of clay or brick, simulated by the cast-iron Dutch oven at the hearth, provided steam automatically because moisture from the loaf was confined in the small space and was turned to steam by the radiant heat of clay, brick, or iron. When a fire was built directly in the oven, the initial heat steamed the crust, and the falling heat gradually cooked the interior of the loaf.

An easy way to provide steam in our modern domestic gas or electric ovens is to spray the loaves with a plant atomizer to get the sharp crust of a French-Italian loaf. Another way is to put a pan partially filled with boiling water into the oven when you preheat it. If you fill the pan only an inch or two, the water will give initial steam but will also evaporate so that the loaf can finish cooking in a relatively dry oven. More simply yet, a glaze of water or milk, or egg mixed with either, brushed over the top of your loaf, will help guarantee a good browned top crust.

The best way to provide radiant heat is to line the oven shelf with a layer of clay tiles or a pizza tile, on which you can put the dough directly if the tile is oiled and sprinkled with a little cornmeal or flour. Because you should heat the tile in the oven when you preheat it, I find it more convenient to put my loaf on a baking sheet (sprinkled with cornmeal) for its final rise, and then to put the sheet on the tile. You can also bake your loaf in a well-greased clay flowerpot or in one of the clay bread ovens sold now through fancy kitchenware outlets. You don't *have* to have any special equipment, of course, not even a bread pan. You can bake dough on a well-greased sheet of aluminum foil or in an empty coffee can, a pie or cake pan, a skillet, or an aluminum pot.

The loaf is done when the bottom crust sounds hollow when rapped with a knuckle. To test it, slip the loaf from its pan and rap it. If the loaf does not sound hollow, you can return it to the oven shelf without its pan to finish the interior and brown the crust with further cooking. When the loaf is hollow-sounding, let it cool on a rack so that the bottom crust will not soften in its own interior steam. An overcooked loaf will simply be a bit dry but will be perfectly edible, while an undercooked loaf will have spots of wet flour in its interior.

Baking times with yeast breads are much more flexible than with cakes or pastries or even quick breads.

KEEPING BREAD

The best way to keep bread is still the old-fashioned tin bread box, which provides space for the loaf to breathe. The second best, and for the same reason, is a paper bag rather than a plastic one. Plastic will keep the bread moist but may soften the crust. Keeping bread in the refrigerator prevents mold, but also hastens the bread's growing stale or drying out. If you find your bread beginning to go stale, slice it and freeze the slices, which will then thaw when toasted.

In any case, toasting or simply reheating bread in an oven will refresh its taste and texture. Bread, cooked or uncooked, freezes extremely well if wrapped first in plastic to prevent air pockets, and then in foil. You can thaw frozen bread at room temperature and then give it a quick refresher for 10 or 15 minutes in a 350° oven. Or you can thaw the loaf entirely in the oven, if you allow 30 to 40 minutes at a lower temperature of 300°.

To make good bread you no longer need to be up at the crack of dawn. With the regulated cold and heat of refrigerators and stoves, you no longer need to worry about the weather. All you need are ministering hands to create the elemental pleasure of a risen loaf.

Sourdough Country Bread from Scratch*

FOR THE STARTER:
1 cup whole-wheat flour
1 cup warm water
2 cups grated raw potato
1/4 cup dried hops (optional)**

FOR THE SPONGE:
1 1/2 cups unbleached flour
1/2 cup lukewarm water
1/2 cup starter

FOR THE DOUGH:
1 tablespoon salt
1 cup warm beer or ale
3–4 cups unbleached flour

Make the starter by mixing the flour, water, potato, and hops in a bowl large enough for the mixture to bubble up. Cover with cheesecloth or a damp kitchen towel and

*Making your own wild yeast takes extra time. Allow about a week for full fermentation of starter, sponge, and dough. You can shorten the process by half by adding a package of dry yeast to your starter and letting it sit for a day before adding it to the sponge.

**Dried hops are available in many herb and health food stores. They are here only for flavor and are not at all necessary to the fermentation. Neither is the potato, but it will speed fermentation because of its high starch content.

let sit at room temperature for 24 hours. Stir mixture down, cover with plastic wrap to hold in the moisture, and let sit for 2 or 3 days. Scoop out ½ cup to make the sponge and preserve the rest in a lidded jar or plastic bag in the freezer.

Make the sponge by mixing the flour, water, and starter. Return mixture to the bowl, cover with cheese-cloth or towel, and let sit for 1 or 2 days (the longer it sits the sourer it gets). To complete the dough, mix the sponge with the salt, beer, and 3 cups of the unbleached flour. Knead the dough by hand for about 10 minutes, or by machine for about 5, adding more flour as needed to keep the dough from being too sticky; but this dough should be soft rather than stiff.

Put the dough in a bowl, cover it, and let it rise for 8–12 hours (it will not double but will rise slightly). Shape the loaf into a large round and place it on a prepared baking sheet (greased and sprinkled with flour or corn-meal). Cover it again with cloth or towel and let sit in a warm place 4–8 hours. Slash the top with a razor blade 3 or 4 times and bake it at 375° for 50–75 minutes. Loaf should sound hollow when rapped on the bottom. Cool loaf on a rack.

Yields 1 large, round loaf about 2 or 3 inches high at the center.

Walnut-Oat Bread

2 packages dry yeast
2 cups very warm milk (105–115°)
2 cups whole-wheat flour
2–3 cups unbleached all-purpose flour
1 tablespoon salt
½ cup oat grits
½ cup bran flakes
⅓ cup walnut oil
1½ cups walnuts, chopped

Dissolve yeast in the milk. Add the whole-wheat flour, 2 cups of the unbleached flour, the salt, oats, and bran. Stir in the oil and mix well. Add the walnuts and knead, adding more unbleached flour as needed, until dough is elastic and glossy. Let dough rise in a warm place (70°–80°) until doubled, about 2 hours (the oil in the dough makes this a slow-rising bread). Punch the dough down with your fist and let the dough rise again. Divide dough in two, pat each ball into a flat circle, indent it in the center with the side of your hand, and fold the dough under to make a high round. Cut a cross in the top of each with a razor blade. Brush tops with a little more walnut oil and let rise on a baking sheet lightly greased and sprinkled with cornmeal. Bake at 400° for 30–45 minutes, or until loaves sound hollow when tapped on the bottom. Cool on a rack.

Yields 2 round loaves.

Sprouted Wheat Bread

TO SPROUT WHEAT BERRIES:
1/2 cup wheat berries
2 cups water

Soak berries in cold water for 12 hours. Drain berries and put them in a quart jar. Cover opening with cheese-cloth and secure it with a rubber band. Turn jar on its side and put it in a dark place for two days. Rinse berries daily by pouring warm water through the cheesecloth and drain-ing it. Sprouts are ready when the shoots are 1/2 inch long.

FOR THE DOUGH:
1/2 cup unsprouted wheat berries
1 package dry yeast
1 1/4 cups warm water (110–115°)
1/4 cup molasses
2 1/2 cups unbleached flour
1 1/2 cups whole-wheat flour
1 cup sprouted wheat berries
2 teaspoons salt
1/4 cup vegetable oil

Soak the unsprouted berries in 1/2 cup hot water for 30 minutes. Dissolve yeast in the warm water in a large mixing bowl. Add molasses and mix well. Add the re-maining ingredients and knead dough until it is smooth and elastic (10–15 minutes by hand or about 5 minutes in an electric mixer with a dough hook). Let dough rise in a plastic bag, floured on the inside, until dough has doubled in volume. Punch the dough down with your fist. Divide dough into two rounds and put on a cookie sheet. Let dough rise again, about 45 minutes. Bake at 375° for 30-40 minutes, or until loaves sound hollow when tapped. Cool on a rack.

Yields 2 small loaves.

Tuscan Herb Bread
(Focaccia)

1 package dry yeast
3/4 cup very warm water (105-115°)
2 3/4 cups unbleached flour
1 tablespoon sea salt
1/2 cup dry vermouth or dry white wine
1/3 cup olive oil
1/4 cup each chopped garlic and fresh rosemary
1/3 cup grated Parmesan cheese
1 tablespoon black pepper

Make a sponge of the yeast, water, and 1 cup of the flour. Cover and let ferment 2-3 hours. Add sponge to remaining flour and mix with 1 teaspoon of the salt, the vermouth, and half the olive oil. Mix in the herbs and cheese and knead dough until it is elastic. Put dough in an oiled bowl, and cover and let rise until doubled (1 1/2-2 hours). Punch dough down with your fist. Pat it into a large circle, about 1/4 inch thick, on a pizza pan or other baking sheet sprinkled with cornmeal. Pour remaining oil on top of the dough and sprinkle top with remaining salt and black pepper. Bake at 475°F for 15-20 minutes, or until loaf sounds hollow when tapped on the bottom. Cool on a rack.

Yields 1 large 15-inch round.

QUICK BREADS

In the beginning all bread was flat. It was flat because it was unleavened. Flat bread presumably began when our primal ancestors discovered that acorns roasted in the ashes of a fire tasted better than acorns raw, and that acorns ground into a paste and then roasted were easier on the teeth and stomach. At some point our Stone Age ancestors must have discovered that stones were good for baking, as well as for cutting, grinding, and clobbering. A hot stone by the campfire could be used as a griddle for cooking a patty of ground acorns moistened with water to hold it together. From such little acorns, big loaves and, indeed, whole forests of bread have grown.

Much of the world still bakes its bread flat on stones or iron griddles because that is the simplest, cheapest, and quickest way to make bread. Where Indians of the Far East make a simple flour-and-water paste of whole wheat, roll it thin, slap it on a griddle, and call it *chapati*, Indians of the Far West make a flour-and-water paste of corn, slap it on an iron copal or a stone piki hearth, and call it *tortilla* or *piki*. While the grains vary greatly, the methods of cooking unleavened bread are surprisingly similar. In contrast to leavened bread, which takes its own sweet time, unleavened bread is invariably quick bread.

Unleavened bread, from Jewish matzo to British biscuit, is also good traveling bread. Baked flour-and-water paste may break your teeth, but it's not apt to mold. For our colonial ancestors, to make a quick bread that would last long and travel far was often a matter of life and death. But such knowledge came hard, for in North America the first explorers were confronted with a grain wholly unlike the glutenous grains of Europe. Colonists long accustomed to yeast-leavened breads made of wheat, rye, barley, and oats had to learn from primitive Indians how to cope with a grain that had no gluten at all and produced a bread that was as flat as the world was round. In the beginning, all American bread was flat because it was made of corn.

GRAINS

The pleasure of unleavened bread is in the taste and texture of the natural grain itself, untransformed by the fermentation that occurs when yeast is added. The way in which the grain is milled also affects flavor and texture. The original Indian corn, or maize, was notably obdurate and had to be dried, parched, or roasted and shelled before it could be ground at all. The Aztecs crushed their maize between a pair of stones, like a stone mortar and pestle, that the Spaniards called *metate* and *mano*. American colonists used hand-powered mills, grinding the dried kernels between stone disks set in a washtub or barrel. Later they built water- and wind-powered grist mills. As with the milling of wheat, this method of milling corn did not change until after the middle of the nineteenth century, when steel rollers supplanted stone grinding wheels in grain mills.

As with wheat, so with corn: a gain in speed and efficiency brought a loss in nutrients and taste, since the rollers split off the germ of the corn kernel, which was then processed separately to produce corn oil. Whole kernel stone-ground cornmeals, found mostly today in health food and specialty stores, taste better than standard commercial meals because they retain the oil-rich germ.

Corn can be milled to give more varied textures than wheat. Dried corn is ground coarsely into grits, more finely into meal, and most finely into flour. While "grits" properly refers to any grain coarsely ground, so that one can have oat grits and barley grits, in America grits have become synonymous with the bleached, skinned corn called hominy. American Indians processed dried corn into hominy by soaking the kernels in lye leached from wood ashes, then removing the loosened skin, and cracking the inner kernels by pounding them.

For flat breads of any grain, where the crunch and earthy taste of the grain are primary, grits are preferable to flour. With oats, steel-cut oat grits are very different from the rolled oats of the familiar American cereal, where the grain is first husked and then flattened between mechanical rollers so that it will cook rapidly. With steel-cut oats, the husked grain is chopped rather than crushed, to produce a distinctive grit used in the traditional Scottish oatcake. Some English have scorned oats as fit for horses and only in Scotland for people, as Dr. Samuel Johnson put it. Because oats have a thick adherent husk with an inner kernel, or groat, of almost no gluten, oats were traditionally used for porridges or flat, gritty oatcakes rather than fine bread.

What oats are to Scotland, Ireland, and much of Central Europe, barley and rye are to Wales and Scandinavia. But as long ago as ancient Rome, all these grains were subject to a class division based on their gluten powers. Low-gluten grains and thus heavy breads were staples for peasants and the poor; high-gluten wheat was food for the rich. Today, with the reverse snobbery endemic to fashion, peasant foods and especially peasant breads have become chic—and with good reason. To get breads of character, we must rediscover the distinctive qualities and capacities of the grains we have so long condemned.

Because barley and rye, for example, contain less fat than oats or corn, bread made of the former tends to be extremely dry. Norwegians take advantage of that "defect" to make wafer-thin breads we label generically "rye-crisp." When crispness and dryness are not wanted, barley or rye cakes and breads are often made with milk instead of water, because the butterfat of milk supplies the fat missing from the grain.

When raised breads are wanted instead of flat ones, finely milled flour rises to the occasion better than coarse grits or meal. Since wheat grinds finer than any other grain, wheat flour has the greatest capacity for rising with leavenings other than yeast. While a firm hand is needed to develop the elastic gluten of a yeasted dough, for a dough without yeast, a light, quick hand is required to mix the flour with air, egg white, or a chemical leavening that either works fast or not at all.

BAKING POWDERS

Bread raised by chemical powders like sodium bicarbonate rather than by yeast are so common today that it may be hard to realize that such breads did not come into vogue until the middle of the nineteenth century. Soda breads were one of our first fast foods, providing the weary housewife with an instant raised bread that required neither expensive eggs nor slow yeast. The substance we now call "baking soda" was a boon to a hard-working peasantry like the Irish, who have given us a number of delicious soda breads. But curiously, the origin of baking soda dates back to the American Indians and their way of making flat corn bread more palatable and digestible.

Indians must have discovered very early that the alkaline properties of wood ash would sweeten, season, and make more nourishing their cakes and breads of corn. Wood ash happens to be rich in the very minerals corn lacks, so that the addition of wood ashes from different kinds of wood to cornmeals of different kinds was common to Indians across the continent. Ashes provided flavor, nutrition, and, if there were any acid present, a certain amount of leavening.

The reaction of alkali with acid produces the same bubbles of carbon dioxide that yeast does. Colonists discovered this reaction when they added a little wood ash to cornmeal or wheat flour moistened with sour milk. Sodium bicarbonate, or "baking soda," is an alkaline related to the potassium bicarbonate of wood ash, which the colonists called "potash." Later, they gentrified the name and the product to "pearl ash." By the end of the eighteenth century, Americans knew that their alkaline pearl ash produced the same bubbling effect with molasses that it did with sour milk and buttermilk. Because of its magical speed, pearl ash became popular with bread makers not only in this country (in 1796 Amelia Simmons, in her *American Cookery*, calls for pearl ash in her "Molasses Gingerbread"), but in Europe as well. In 1792 America shipped some 8,000 tons of pearl ash to the Old World.

As techniques of refinement progressed, pearl ash was replaced by "saleratus," which was simply a salt such as potassium or sodium bicarbonate that had been aerated. By 1856 the introduction of a commercial premixed "baking powder" eliminated the need for mixing baking soda with a separate acid ingredient. Now an acid powder—a tartrate, phosphate, or sulfate—was mixed with the alkaline powder and a little cornstarch in order to keep the powder dry.

Housewives took to baking powder like mice to cheese. Rival manufacturers, eager to corner the new market, advertised their own mixture as "pure" and their rivals' as "poisonous." The baking powder wars had begun. Because some acids act faster than others, most commercial brands of baking powder today combine a pair of acids. "Double-acting" baking powders contain two different acid salts, one of which acts at room temperature, the other at a heated oven temperature. Cream of tartar and monocalcium phosphate are both common fast-acting salts; sodium aluminum sulfate is the most common delayed-action, or high-temperature, salt. From a cook's point of view, there are two gas releases: the first when the powder comes in contact with a liquid and the second when the resulting mixture comes in contact with heat.

You can easily make your own single-acting baking powder by mixing (for each cup of flour) 1 teaspoon cream of tartar to ½ teaspoon baking soda. Cream of tartar is a rather fanciful name for a product derived from wine dregs, or tartaric acid. Without baking powder you can get the same carbon dioxide by mixing ¼ teaspoon baking soda with ½ cup sour milk. To get sour milk you can sour sweet milk by adding a tablespoon of lemon juice or vinegar to a cup of warm milk and letting it stand for 10 to 15 minutes, until it begins to curdle. Curdled milk will have the sourness but not the richness of buttermilk. If you want buttermilk and have none, yoghurt will substitute.

When recipes call for both baking powder and baking soda, the additional soda is there not for leavening but for neutralizing an acid taste. Some recipes may call for baking soda alone, because the presence of an acid ingredient renders unnecessary the additional acid in baking powder. As with other bread recipes, in quick breads proportion is all. You can adjust the chemical effects on taste and texture to the requirements of your own palate. Once again, the only rule is to experiment.

EGGS

Before baking soda or powder inaugurated the modern age of quick baking, breads without yeast were raised chiefly by the addition of eggs. Because of the capacity of egg whites to expand when air is beaten into them, batters could be leavened slightly when whole eggs were well beaten before adding them. But if yolks and whites were beaten separately before adding, a batter might rise to astonishing heights. By the late sixteenth century, the English were leavening pound cakes, biscuit breads, and "fine breads" with whole eggs "beaten together for two hours." By the eighteenth century eggs had come to replace yeast in traditional seed cakes and plum or fruit cakes. But eggs were far more costly than yeast in both time and money. Once chemical powders were introduced into baking, eggs were a luxury reserved for festal breads or cakes and for conspicuous consumption.

In contrast to peasant flat breads, chemically raised breads became a symbol of social and even sexual status in America in the late-nineteenth and early-twentieth centuries. Flat breads rose to ever new heights, and cookbooks swelled with elegant variations of baking powder biscuits, rolls, and cakes, as homesteaders laid down their guns and took up plowshares and bake ovens. Aeration became a sign of civilization and of female encroachment on territory once staked out by men.

The evolution of Southern spoon bread is a good example of how a former he-man corn pone turned into an effete cornmeal soufflé. In early-nineteenth-century recipes, corn bread is leavened only by the action of bicarbonate of soda on buttermilk. Later recipes added whole eggs. Today, a standard spoon bread recipe separates the eggs and increases their number to turn the homely grit into an upwardly mobile and ladylike pudding or cake.

The British tea scone stands similarly high on the culinary social ladder in relation to lowly soda breads and even lower oat or barley cakes. The scone reveals its upper-class status by the addition of both baking powder and whole eggs to make a plebeian biscuit at once lighter and richer.

The transformation of flat breads by baking powders coincided with the transformation of the open hearth by enclosed wood and coal stoves in which to bake them. A heated hoe, a hot brick, an iron skillet, a Dutch oven, or other improvised "bake kettle" was useful for peasant and pioneer living, but less so for producing the delicate refinements of the tea table. As a metal stove that incorporated an oven stood literally higher than a griddle or a hearth, so raised bread suggested social elevations unknown to the makers of flat bread.

At the fag end of the industrial revolution, as we look back with nostalgia to earlier and simpler ways, we may rediscover virtues in coarser and flatter breads. Pampered by instant fires and instant powders, we may still experience with our palates and our hands the force of those ancient grains that sustained life when men without cities made bread without yeast.

American Egg Corn Pone

2 cups yellow corn grits or hominy grits
1 teaspoon salt
2 cups boiling water
2 eggs, well beaten
6 tablespoons leaf lard, bacon fat, or butter

Mix grits with salt and stir them slowly into the boiling water. Mix in the eggs. Heat the lard in a 12-inch heavy cast-iron or ovenproof skillet. Pour the corn batter into the hot fat and bake at 425° for 25–30 minutes, or until the top is well browned. Serve hot with lots of butter. Yields a 12-inch round pone about 1 inch thick.

Scottish Oatcakes

1 cup toasted oat grits (steel-cut)
1 cup oat flour, oatmeal, or rolled oats
1¼ teaspoons salt
2 tablespoons butter
1¼ cups boiling water

Mix grits, flour, and salt. (You can make oatmeal from grits or rolled oats by putting a cup of the oats in a blender and processing at top speed for 30 seconds or more.) Melt butter with the boiling water and stir into the dry ingredients. On a pair of ungreased baking sheets, spoon out sixteen lumps of dough and flatten each to make a thin round 3 inches in diameter and ¹⁄16 inch thick.

Bake at 300° for about an hour, or until the cakes are golden brown. Serve with butter and a strong cheese like Stilton.

Yields about sixteen 3-inch cakes.

English Cream Scones

4 cups unbleached white flour
1/4 cup sugar
1 teaspoon salt
2 teaspoons baking powder
3/4 pound (3 sticks) butter, chilled
4 eggs, beaten
1 1/2 cups heavy cream
1 cup golden raisins

Preheat oven to 375°. Mix dry ingredients. Cut butter into 8 slices per stick and rub it into the flour with your fingertips, cut it in with knives, or use the pulse action of a food processor. Beat the eggs into the cream and fork the liquid lightly into the flour. Do not overmix or you will toughen the dough. Fold in the raisins. Shape dough on a floured surface into a rectangle about 1 inch thick. Cut it into triangles or squares and put them on lightly buttered baking sheets. Bake at 375° for 20-25 minutes. Serve hot with additional butter or whipped cream and strawberry jam.

Yields 16-24 scones.

Irish Whole-Wheat Soda Bread

3 cups whole-wheat flour
1 cup unbleached white flour
1½ teaspoons salt
1 teaspoon baking soda
1¾ cups buttermilk, sour milk, or yoghurt*

Grease a baking sheet or an 8-inch cake pan. Preheat oven to 475°. Mix the dry ingredients thoroughly, then stir in the liquid and knead gently two or three minutes with your fingertips. Shape dough into a high round; the dough will spread slightly. Cut a deep cross on top of the loaf with a razor blade, so that you can divide the bread into quarters after it is baked. To help the dough rise, invert a deep cake pan, metal mold, or ovenproof bowl over the loaf for the first 10 minutes of baking. Then remove the inverted pan to brown the crust. Lower oven to 400° and bake another 20–45 minutes, or until the loaf sounds hollow when tapped on the bottom. Butter lavishly and eat hot.

Yields one 8-inch loaf.

*For a sweet soda bread, add 2 tablespoons sugar to the dry ingredients and a cup of raisins or currants after the buttermilk.

Finnish Barley Bread

2 cups barley grits*
1 teaspoon salt
2 teaspoons baking powder
4 tablespoons butter
1 cup light cream

Mix dry ingredients thoroughly. Preheat oven to 450°. Melt butter in a 14-inch cast-iron or nonstick skillet and add half the butter to the grits. Stir in the cream and pour the batter into the remaining butter in the hot skillet. Smooth the batter to make a flat bread about ½ inch thick. Bake at 450° for 20–30 minutes, or until the top of the bread is lightly browned. (Because of the grayish-white color of barley, the bread becomes an unusual grayish-tan when it is browned.)

Yields one 14-inch round loaf.

*If you can't find barley grits at a health-food store, put standard pearl barley grains into a blender and process at top speed.

INDEX

A NOTE ABOUT THE AUTHOR

Betty Fussell is a Californian who now makes her home in New York City. She has written regularly for publications ranging from *The New York Times* and *Vogue* to the *Journal of Gastronomy* and *Country Journal,* and is the author of *I Hear America Cooking, Eating In, Masters of American Cookery,* and *Mabel: Hollywood's First I-Don't-Care Girl.*

A NOTE ON THE TYPE

The text of this book was set on the Linotype in Century Expanded, a type designed in 1894 by Linn Boyd Benton (1844–1932). Benton cut Century Expanded in response to a request by Theodore L. De Vinne for an attractive, easy-to-read type face to fit the narrow columns of his *Century Magazine.* Early in the 1900s Benton's son, Morris Fuller Benton, updated and improved Century in several versions for his father's American Type Founders Company. Century remains the only American type face cut before 1910 that is still widely in use today.

Composed by Superior Type, Champaign, Illinois

Printed and bound by Halliday Lithographers,
West Hanover, Massachusetts

Design by Dorothy Schmiderer Baker